TENNIS -- EVERYONE

Clancy Moore
and
M.B. Chafin

University of Florida
Gainesville, Florida

H HUNTER PUBLISHING COMPANY

The authors would like to express deep appreciation to several individuals who assisted in the writing of this book. Sincere thanks are in order to Mike Chafin, who spent many hours on the courts as the subject of the illustrations, to Melissa Floyd, for allowing the use of modeling photographs, and P.A. Lee for demonstrations concerning officiating. The authors are also grateful to Mike Floyd, owner of Court Side Sports, for allowing the use of his well equipped tennis shop, and to Evelyn Boring for clerical and typing skills.

Printed in the United States of America
Hunter Publishing Company, Winston-Salem, North Carolina

Second Printing, 1980

CONTENTS

Opposite: (Top) Mixed doubles circa 1910. (Bottom) Davis Cup, 1912, Australia versus Great Britain.

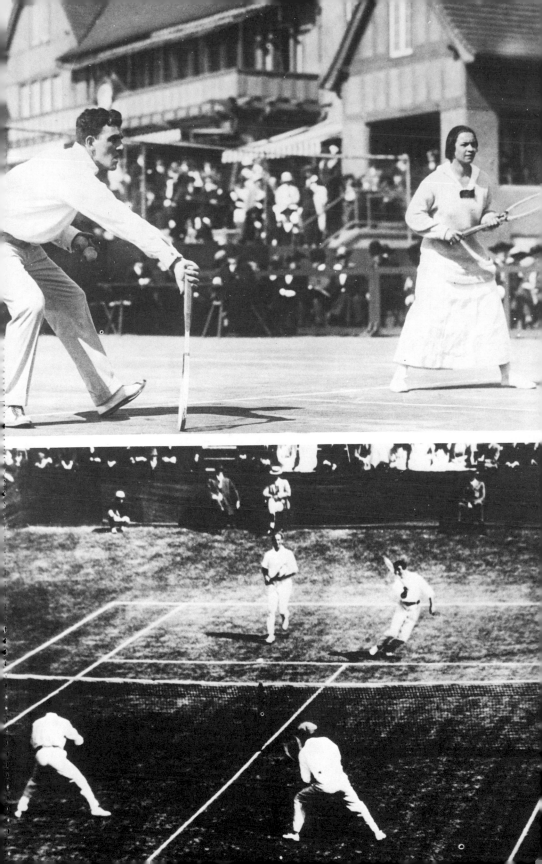

CHAPTER 1

TENNIS — TODAY AND YESTERDAY

WHY TENNIS?

At this point you are probably asking yourself, "Why did I choose tennis?" Or perhaps you are already a "sometimes" player and are asking the question, "Why do I continue to play this crazy, frustrating game?"

Whatever your reason, it is possible that in the next few weeks you will arrive at a decision which will affect your lifestyle and habits for the remainder of your life. However, if by chance you should decide that the game of tennis is not for you, at least the decision will be made on the basis of sound information and a fair trial.

As a non-contact sport tennis offers a wide range of diverse benefits to all participants. First and foremost the game is one of motor skill requiring a strong emphasis on hand-eye coordination with a corresponding emphasis on speed, strength, endurance, and agility. This in no way minimizes that the ability to correctly stroke a tennis ball is fundamental to long-range success. Of equal importance is a mental aspect to the game that is not found in many other athletic endeavors. It is impossible to be a winning tennis player and not be reasonably intelligent. Additionally you must possess the ability to calculate while engaged in a fiercely contested point. It has been said that perhaps the mental involvement of tennis requires more from its participants than any other sport.

While many tennis matches have been decided on the durability of their performers, one of the best aspects of the game is that it can be adapted to the participant's age, sex, and level of competition. Like checker players, older participants frequently develop a seasoned degree of "gamesmanship" which offers some compensation for legs that may have lost their spring. Then there is always the doubles game which can be enjoyed as long as a person can maintain some degree of mobility. Tennis, as some other sports, also has its own handicapping system. Should you feel you are too accomplished to play with someone, try beginning each game with a one- or two-point deficit and see how quickly the competition is evened!

In terms of a fitness activity, tennis is decidedly better for you than most other sports. Discounting running and swimming which burn more calories, but which are boring and repetitious, tennis probably offers more advantages than any other activity. Approximately 40 million people in the United States alone have decided that the idea of burning up to 500 calories an hour, increasing muscle strength without a great increase in muscle size, releasing tension in a wholesome manner, and socializing both for business and pleasure are definitely to their liking. To top it all off, most agree tennis is fun; therefore, it is their answer to the current fitness drive.

Another aspect of tennis which has remained through the years is the capacity for developing true sportsmanship despite the intense competetive nature of the game. The cheating tennis player is an oddity rather than the rule, and whenever players do not conform to the unwritten code, they are quickly abandoned by other players.

In addition, tennis is found and played throughout the world, and the nature of the game is such that both sexes can compete with and against each other.

By this time you may be convinced that tennis is the game for you and you are anxious to get on the courts. However, there are several points which must be stated so as not to create false illusions.

First of all, tennis need not cost a lot of money. If you choose to join a private club, play at night or indoors, and purchase the most expensive equipment, the cost could amount to a considerable sum of money. However, if you play on public courts and select moderately priced equipment, the game will cost considerably less than golf, skiing, or boating.

There is another word of caution, and that concerns the mastery of the game. Tennis does require a commitment of time if you really want to improve your level of skills. Unfortunately it is not one of the easiest games to master. However, almost everyone who perseveres can become reasonably adept at stroking the ball. They may not look and play like professional players but they will derive many of the same benefits which keep most tennis players returning to the courts year after year. Another caution, "once hooked" you will probably play the game for the rest of your life.

ORIGIN OF THE GAME

The history of ancient civilizations indicates that a form of tennis was probably played by the early Greeks and Romans. Other evidence indicates that the Chinese were batting a ball back and forth more than 7,000 years ago, and that the Egyptians and Persians also played some kind of a ball and racket game as early as 500 B.C.

The most solid and recent evidence, however, indicates a tennis-like game being played in France about 1200 A.D. The French game called "jeu de paume," or game of the hand, consisted of hitting a stuffed object over a rope with the bare hand. Rackets did not make an appearance until about 1400 A.D. England and Holland had both accepted the sport by this time and Chaucer referred to the game by using the present name, which is probably a derivative of the French word "Ten-ez."

The game prospered greatly in France and

England. However, the French Revolution almost obliterated the sport since at that time it was considered a game of the rich.

One must remember that this earliest contest did not much resemble our present game. It was not until 1873 that a British army major by the name of Walter C. Wingfield introduced a new outdoor game which, while incorporating many of the older aspects, was more similar to our present grass court game. He chose to name his game "Sphairistike," a Greek word meaning "to play." Since the name was too difficult to pronounce, let alone spell, the English quickly began calling the game "tennis on the lawn" and eventually lawn tennis.

The game quickly spread throughout the British empire, and in the year 1874 Miss Mary Outerbridge, who was vacationing in Bermuda, brought the game with her to New York. As a member of the Staten Island Cricket Club, she quickly received permission to lay out a court on an unused portion of the cricket grounds.

Although the game was not an overnight success in America, it was only a few years before every major club in the East had courts. Since there was little standardization in these early years, with each club having its own rules, conflicts gradually arose. Finally in 1881, an older brother of Mary Outerbridge convened a meeting of the leading New York clubs to bring some order to the then existing confusion. The outcome of his meeting was the establishment of the United States Lawn Tennis Association, which later became the United States Tennis Association.

The first United States Championship was held in Newport, Rhode Island, that same year and was won by Richard Sears, who subsequently defended and held his title for the next six years. In 1915, the tournament was permanently moved to the West Side Tennis Club in Forest Hills, Long Island, and was held there through 1977. In 1978, the tournament was moved to Flushing Meadows, New York.

At approximately the same time, another tournament of tremendous importance was being inaugurated at Wimbledon, England.

The Davis Cup

The subsequent elegance and tradition has established this tournament as perhaps the most important tournament in the world.

A few years later in 1884, Wimbledon began its annual tournament for women, and as the ladies gradually began to shed their voluminous clothing their game became indistinguishable from that of the men.

The Davis Cup, one of the most prestigious awards in tennis, was originated by Dwight Davis, who, while still a student at Harvard, donated a cup to be awarded to the winner of a team match between England and the United States. Today this competition has grown to include teams from all over the world and has contributed greatly to world understanding among tennis players.

CHAPTER 1 EVALUATION

1. What are the motor skills necessary to participate actively in tennis? Explain the importance of each with specific reference to tennis.

2. Why is tennis so popular as an all-round sport to cause 40 million participants to seek opportunities for play annually?

3. The average tennis player can expend how many calories per hour in competition?

4. From a historical viewpoint, tennis can be traced back to the cultures of two areas of civilization. Who were they?

5. The oldest evidence of a racket and ball type game is from which country?

6. Our game of tennis has its positive development in France about 1200 A.D. What was it called in those days?

7. What did the word "Sphairistike" mean, and who developed it? Who named our game "lawn tennis"?

8. Tennis was brought to the U.S. by a lady who learned the game in Bermuda. The year was 1874. What was her name?

9. The U.S.L.T.A. first began in the year_____. What does U.S.L.T.A. stand for? It has since changed to the_____which stands for
_____

10. The first U.S. Championship was held in 1881 and was won by _____

11. What are the three locations of the United States championships to date?

12. What is the most important championship tennis tournament in the world? Where is it held?

13. International competition for men representing their respective countries is the_____.

CHAPTER 2

EQUIPMENT AND FACILITIES

BUYING YOUR EQUIPMENT

How much should I spend on a tennis racket? One thing is certain. It is **not** necessary for a beginner to buy a name brand product and spend more than $20-$25 for a racket. As you improve your game, begin to observe other players' rackets and occasionally ask to hit a few balls with the various models. This is the only way to determine the true "feel" of a racket and what seems best for you. Many pro shops and dealers now offer prospective customers the opportunity of hitting with different types of rackets.

What do the various markings on the handle of my racket mean? If you have markings it probably indicates that you have a quality racket. The numbers and letters themselves usually indicate handle size, weight of frame, and sometimes special model numbers. Handle sizes are indicated by the numbers 4⅜ 4½, 4⅝, and 4¾ and indicate the circumference of the handle in inches. Racket weight will be designated by either the letters L, M, or H immediately following the handle size as, 4⅜ L. The letters indicate a range in ounces which may vary among manufacturers but L (light) rackets usually weight less than 13-14 ounces. H (heavy) rackets will weigh more than 14 ounces and M (medium) rackets will range somewhere in between the two.

But what about me — what size and weight should I have? At this point in your tennis career it is impossible to say with certainty. However, there are several rule of thumb measurements and generalizations which may assist you in your initial choice.

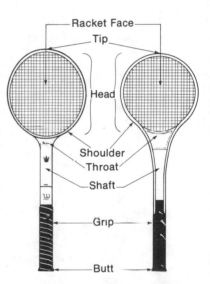

If you will shake hands with a racket handle the tip of your thumb should be able to touch the first joint of your middle finger. Also, the average grip sizes for women is usually 4 1/2 and for men 4 5/8. However, if your hands are unusually large or small for your sex this would have to be adjusted to your particular case.

What about the racket weight? In general, adult women should begin with the 13-14 ounce range and men should begin with a racket of medium weight. Of course your physique and strength will greatly influence the weight most appropriate for you. Many tennis professionals feel that a slightly heavier racket aids the rhythm of the swing, and it is important for the beginner to "groove a swing" as early as possible. Lighter rackets are supposed to improve one's touch or feel, and it is true that the great "Little Mo" Connolly preferred a racket of less than 13 ounces. Some rackets are "head heavy" or slightly heavier in the head than in the handle and are usually preferred by baseline players.

Others who play a great amount of doubles or who volley a lot seem to prefer a "handle heavy" racket. Racket weight, like baseball players' bats, is a very personal thing and can only be determined after you have had ample time to experiment.

I have heard a lot about flex or flexibility in rackets. Is this important? In general, wooden rackets are stiffer than metal rackets, but there is a wide range of differences within each category. As with tightly strung strings, metal, or very flexible rackets, tend to provide more power but less control. A more loosely strung racket and a stiffer frame will give a player less power but more control. From a beginner's standpoint, **control** is far more important than speed.

A friend of mine has offered me a "used" racket. How can I tell if it is a "quality" racket? The first thing to do is to examine the frame for warping and cracks, or if a metal frame, look for flex cracking and dents. Wooden rackets tend to crack first in the extreme bottom and top positions of the racket head. The handle should be of good quality leather and not have staples or nails exposed to sight. The head of the racket should contain seven to twelve laminations as do more expensive rackets. If the racket is metal, is the welding and riveting secure? the general workmanship and finish will also provide some indication of quality. Also, do not forget that many of the better rackets have permanent markings on the side of the racket indicating size and weight.

Do I need a racket cover and press? Racket covers are good for all types of rackets. A dash of talcum powder placed within the cover and a gentle slap after the racket has been replaced will protect both strings and frame from collecting moisture. Good quality wooden frames should not require a press; however, the use of a press on a wooden racket prevents any possibility of warping.

There are so many different kinds of racket strings, which should I buy? First of all many rackets are sold with factory strings. These are usually mono-filament, multi-ply or pro-fected nylon. All are fairly durable, and usually are strung at about 40 pounds pressure. While advanced players usually prefer strings at 50-60 pounds of tension, many pros feel that 45-52 pounds is more advantageous to beginners since control is more important than speed.

Gut strings, which are the most expensive, and are the most affected by moisture, offer the advantage of increased hitting power. Of course for the beginner this may not be an asset since increased resiliency frequently means decreased accuracy. One word of caution — if you chop the ball often and use a hard slice serve you may wish to use a very good grade of nylon or a synthetic string of some hardness. Also, there are commercial sprays (usually shellac) which will increase the life of strings, but tend to decrease their resiliency.

How many times can my racket be restrung? This depends upon the initial quality of your racket and how you take care of it. A reasonable expectation would be four to six times over a period of two or three years. Repeated stringing of wooden rackets will frequently cause the strings to cut deeply into the frame, particularly at the top of the racket. So check this area closely.

What about size of strings? Strings are usually purchased in 15-16 and 17 gauge thicknesses. The higher the gauge the thinner the string. Therefore, the 17 gauge string would give more hitting power, but the least durability.

What kind of tennis balls should I buy? Tennis balls are as varied as automobiles. In this case it is probably wise to stick to better known name brands such as Wilson, Penn, Dunlop, Spalding and Slazenger. Costs will vary but usually range from $2 to $4 per can of three. Players who play on firm abrasive surfaces as rough concrete or asphalt will realize some savings if they purchase only heavy duty

balls which have an extra heavy covering of felt. Tennis ball quality is determined by standardized requirements, and manufacturers who meet this standard will display a "USTA Approved" stamp on their merchandise.

Most manufacturers inflate their balls with compressed air or gas and pack them in pressurized containers. As you open a new can you should hear a pronounced hissing sound which indicates that the pressure has been maintained. Once opened, balls rapidly lose their resiliency. Should you open a can and not hear this sound, simply return your purchase and most retailers will gladly exchange the can for you. Also, any ball that cracks or breaks early in play should be returned for replacement. One way to quickly check a set of opened balls is to squeeze them for firmness and to drop for bounce. Any ball that appears unusually soft or does not bounce at least knee high has probably lost its compression. Heavily worn balls tend to become unduly light, and some balls that become shaggy in wear tend to collect moisture during play thus becoming very "heavy" and slow. Even new unopened tennis balls that are stored for several months tend to lose some of their vitality.

Must I buy special clothing to play tennis? This depends upon where you choose to play and how important conformity is to you. Tennis players have probably been brainwashed more than any other sports persons as to proper attire. It is true that many private clubs have strict written and unwritten rules governing the dress of court participants. Certainly whether you wear a pair of basketball or track shorts rather than tennis shorts is not going to influence the quality of your game unless you feel self-conscious. What is important is that a person wear light colored clothing and a head covering if playing in intense heat. Also, whatever you choose to wear should be comfortable to you. Many synthetics, while holding an excellent press, do not have absorbant qualities, thus causing great discomfort to wearers. Cotton remains one of the best fabrics for tennis attire.

Tennis shoes may be one exception to the above. Certainly if you play on any soft surface such as clay or rubico you must have relatively smooth soled sneakers and no heels. Basketball or jogging shoes are not suitable since their soles are too deeply indented and leave court marks. If you are to enjoy the game it is a necessity that your feet be reasonably well cared for. This means that if you play on a very hard surface you should have cushioned insoles for better comfort. Leather topped shoes offer a little additional support but tend to cause more sweating since they do not have "breathing" ability. They are also more expensive.

Tennis socks are equally important since they can easily affect the condition of one's feet. For most comfort they should be a mixture of cotton and wool and have great absorbant qualities. Many tennis players always wear two pairs of socks to facilitate this.

Warm up suits or jackets are necessary for comfort if one moves from a hot court to indoor air conditioning or if one chooses to play on cold windy days.

Wristlets and sweat bands are very convenient and necessary if one plays a vigorous game in hot humid climates.

THE TENNIS COURT

While tennis court dimensions are standardized by the governing agencies of tennis, court composition and court settings are as varied as tennis players themselves. In general, types of courts will be determined by climate and area of the country. Most good courts do have some standardized features, however. First of all they will be laid out on a North-South line to minimize sun problems, and they will usually be surrounded by large hedges and/or a green plastic saran fencing to further decrease the effects of wind and to increase ball visibility.

SOFT COURTS

The South probably has a higher proportion of soft courts than any other area of the United States. The most common materials are clay, rubico, and Har-tru. Soft courts have the advantage of being easy on the feet and legs. In addition, the style of play is slower, the ball tends to "sit up" more and the speed will be taken off of the "big hitter." Soft courts tend to favor a soft hitter and to diminish the attacking player's game.

The primary disadvantage of soft surfaces is the difficulty of keeping them in good playing condition. They must be swept, watered, and rolled daily. Also, a freezing climate will cause the court lines to pull out of the ground, and should players be allowed to use a recently thawed or very wet court, damage can easily

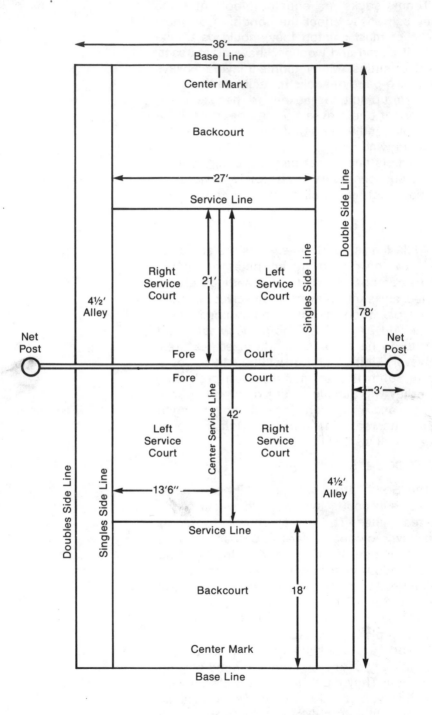

occur which might take weeks to repair. Some porous types, however, do have the advantage of quickly absorbing a hard summer shower and being ready for play in less than an hour.

HARD COURTS

Hard courts of asphalt, wood, composition materials, and cement are more common to the United States than other parts of the world. The Western states have traditionally emphasized this type of court. This surface has a number of advantages with a minimum amount of upkeep being the most prominent feature. Other assets include a uniform ball bounce and increased visibility.

The primary disadvantage of hard surfaces is the wear and tear induced upon a player's feet, legs and shoes. Of course the pace of play is generally much faster since the ball rebounds quickly from this type of surface, thus favoring the driving hitter and big server. However, the surface of a hard court can be modified by the contractor to provide slow, medium or fast play.

NETS AND ACCESSORIES

Tennis nets are generally made of synthetic materials such as nylon, or polyethylene to restrict the effects of moisture. Manufacturers employing the use of cotton or natural fibers generally dip their nets in a creosote-tar substance to retard the rotting process. Metal nets, while durable, have a tendency to bow in or out, thus creating inaccuracies in net height and distance from the net to the baseline. Center straps are necessary on all but metal nets since it is very difficult to achieve a fine adjustment with the windlass found on the net post.

CHAPTER 2 EVALUATION

1. How does one determine the proper handle size and weight of the racket?

2. What are the various playing qualities of strings and tightness or looseness in stringing?

3. Contrast the advantages and disadvantages of soft courts vs hard courts.

4. Contrast the quality of flexibility in tennis rackets. What are the advantages and disadvantages of racket flex?

5. What qualities should tennis clothing possess?

CHAPTER 3

SCORING AND PLAYING THE GAME

First of all it helps greatly if you know the rules. However, these are often written in a technical language and specific points are often hard to find when needed. In addition, there are a number of "unwritten" rules, which, while not specifically covered by the rules book, are nontheless very important to the game and of course to you. See Chapter 15 for the complete Rules of Tennis.

From a teaching standpoint the following questions and points of procedure seem to be the most relevant and are most asked by beginners:

What is a game and how do I keep score?
The points are
No points or 0 = Love
One point = 15
Two points = 30
Three points = 40
Four points = game if two points ahead of opponent

If the players' scores are even after six or more points in a game, the score is referred to as deuce. Should the server go ahead by one point after deuce the score becomes Advantage Server or "Add in," and should the server win the next point it is "Game." However, if the score is tied after six or more points and the receiver wins the next point after deuce then the score becomes Advantage Receiver or "Add-out." If the receiver wins the next point it becomes his or her "Game."

What is a set? A set is a part of a match that is completed when a person or team wins at least six games and is ahead by at least two games as 6-1; 6-2; 6-3; 6-4; 7-5; 8-6 etc. If the "tie breaker" has been elected prior to the match then whoever wins the tiebreaker is awarded that set by a score of 7-6.

What is a tie breaker? The tie breaker is a fairly recent innovation that is used to complete a set when the game score becomes 6-6. This prevents long drawn out contests which may be detrimental to players.

The most commonly used tie breaker is the nine-point tie breaker or best five of nine points. In singles play if player A is due to serve the next regular game, A serves two points, as in normal play starting from the right side. Then the serve goes to the other side with player B doing the same. After these four points the players change sides and the service again goes to player A, who serves the next two points. If a winner has not yet been determined the serve again goes to player B, and B serves two points. At this time, should the score be tied at four all, player B serves point nine. However, A, who is the receiver, may elect to receive the serve from either right or left service court. The players do not change courts after the set and player B begins serving the first game of the new set.

In doubles, let us assume that team A-B is playing team C-D; A and C serve the first four points, sides are changed, and B-D serve the next four. Should a ninth point be necessary, player D serves the third serve. Remember, players always must serve from the same side they have been serving from.

Then who wins the contest or match? Most competitive matches are determined by whoever wins the first two out of three sets. However, some prestigious matches and tournaments are determined by the best three out of five sets.

Are balls that hit the boundary line good? Yes.

What is a let serve and how many times can a person have a let serve? A let serve occurs when a serve hits the top of the net and falls into the proper service area. There is no limit to the number of let serves a person may have.

Balls that hit boundary lines are good.

What if a point other than a serve hits the top of the net and falls into my opponent's court? It is a great shot on your part, and must be returned by your opponent.

If I make a poor toss on the serve, can I catch the ball rather than trying to hit it? Yes, but it is a fault if you swing and miss.

What if my opponent allows the ball from a previous point to remain on his court and I hit the ball during a succeeding rally? It is a great shot on your part and your point if the correct ball is not returned.

Can I throw my racket at the ball and hit it? No.

My doubles partner has a pitty-pat serve and I am getting killed trying to play the net when he serves. What should I do? My first advice would be to get a new partner. However, since this may not be practical, I would suggest backing up to the baseline, at least on all second serves.

My partner does not see very well and returns serves that are frequently faults. Is it legal for me to call serves directed to him, out? Yes, it is your responsibility.

In doubles, can the best serving partner serve first at the beginning of each set? Yes, this is generally a good idea unless the sun or wind causes unusual problems for your partner.

What is a pro-set? A pro-set is when one person or team wins at least eight games and is ahead by at least two games. Example: 8-0; 8-1; 8-2 etc.

Who keeps the score? One of the nice things about tennis is that players usually keep their own score. Other than some tournaments where the umpire will call out the score, it is usually the servers responsibility to call out the score.

Can a player touch the net or reach over the net to hit the ball? A player may not touch the net while play is in progress and may not reach over the net unless the ball has first bounced on his side and then been carried back across by the wind or severe backspin.

Who serves first in a match? It is customary to flip a coin or spin the racket. The winner has the choice of serving, receiving, or choice of court. The loser has the remaining choice.

What if a ball rolls across my court while a point is being played? A let or replay is in order if it is immediately called for. Do not wait until you see whether you win or lose the point before calling "Let."

Can I serve the ball underhanded? Yes.

Can I have some rest in a two out of three set match? Technically no, in men's competition. However, in informal play it is fairly common. In female competition there may be a 10-minute rest period between the second and third set.

What is a foot fault? A foot fault occurs whenever the server makes contact on or within the baseline before hitting the ball. The offending player loses that opportunity to put the ball in play.

Do players ever change ends of the court? Yes, at the completion of games 1,3,5,7,9 etc., in each set.

What happens if I allow a ball to hit me or I catch it while I am outside of the court? This is technically illegal and must be considered a good shot for your opponent even though it is obviously an out shot. Always let the ball go to prevent hassles.

Can I yell or deliberately distract my opponent like I do in basketball and football? No.

What if I blinked just as my opponent's shot hit the court and I was not sure whether it was in or out? Always give your opponent the benefit of doubt. Do not play the ball and then call it out. Remember that each player is responsible for calling out balls on their side of the court.

A foot fault

What if I am forced to leave the court entirely to return a shot, and hit the shot around the net post rather than directly over the net? If the ball lands in your opponent's court you have made a fine shot.

What if the ball just barely touches me during a point? You lose the point.

What if you are playing someone who is obviously cheating you? The best solution is to not play with the person. There are other alternatives, however. You could request an umpire if it is a tournament match, or you could ask for a replay of a certain point.

I entered a tournament and had to play a very long match right off the bat. Luckily I won, but then the tournament director informed me that I could rest 15 minutes and then would have to play my second match? Is this legal? Unfortunately yes. The usual practice, however, is to not require a person to play more than one match in the morning and one in the afternoon. Unfortunately it does not always work out that way. Please read Chapter 14 on Conditioning For Tennis.

How much time do I have between games when changing ends of the court? Technically one minute. However most people do not complain if you towel off, take a drink and wipe your glasses. They have a right to complain if you repair your racket or decide to change socks and shirt.

I sometimes play indoors and my opponent's lobs sometimes hit the lights because of a low ceiling. He always insists on replaying the point. What should I do? He is flimflamming you. If a shot hits an obstruction, whoever hits the ball last loses the point.

In doubles, can my partner and I change sides of the court to receive a serve? No. You must wait until the beginning of a new set.

The person I compete with frequently "quick serves" me? What can I do? Quick

serving is illegal. However, if you swing at the ball it is assumed you were ready. Do not swing at the ball, tell him you were not ready, and suggest that he, "Take two, please."

I sometimes play with this guy who is better than I am and he always wants to rally to see who serves first? If I were better than you and could get you to agree to this, I would too. Tell him the rules say to either spin or flip for choice of serve.

Another guy I play with always wants to begin play on the "first serve in." Is this legal? No.

Spinning the racket for choice of serve

POINTS OF PLAYER AND SPECTATOR ETIQUETTE

1. Before beginning a match always introduce yourself to your partner and opponents.
2. Always check net height at the beginning of a match. One convenient way is to take two standard rackets and stand one on end with the head of the other on top. See Picture page 17.
3. Take all practice serves before playing any points.
4. As a server, do not begin serving any point unless you have two balls at the ready.
5. Failure to observe the foot fault rule will cost you friends.
6. Call lets and faults out in a loud clear voice. A point of the finger upward or sideward will also reinforce a voice call.
7. Never "quick serve" an opponent.
8. Never give unsolicited advice and restrict comments to the conduct of the game.
9. Control emotions and temper.
10. If your ball rolls onto an adjacent court, wait until their point is over then shout, "Thank you, please?"
11. When returning a ball to another court wait until their points are played and they are looking at you.
12. Return only served balls that are good.
13. Do not make excuses. If you lose, you lose, and always shake hands with your opponent.
14. Do not lean on the net to retrieve a ball.
15. If you must cross an occupied court to reach yours, wait until their point or game has been completed.
16. Hit any shot requested by your opponent during the warm up period.
17. Do call a "let" whenever another ball enters your court and return it to its owner.
18. Do keep score accurately.
19. Do give the benefit of the doubt on close calls to your opponent.
20. Do be on time for your match.
21. Do dress properly according to local custom.
22. Do announce the score when you are serving.
23. Never boo a player.
24. Applaud good shots.
25. No moving while the ball is in play.
26. No loud talking or yelling when ball is in play.
27. Do allow the umpire or players to call the match. They are in a much better position than you to call most shots.
28. Do not ask a spectator whether a shot was in or out.

29. Never hit a ball directly at an opponent except during official time in play.
30. Never monopolize the courts.
31. Never wear basketball or jogging shoes on a soft surface court.

TENNIS TERMS

ACE: A perfect serve that is hit beyond the reach of one's opponent.

AD: A shortened word for advantage which refers to the next point after the score is deuce.

AD IN: The score when a serving player wins the next point following deuce.

AD OUT: The score when a receiving player wins the next point following deuce.

ADVANTAGE: The next point after deuce.

ALL: Denotes a tie score as 30-all meaning 30-30.

ALLEY: A 4 1/2 foot lane on both sides of the singles court and necessary for doubles play.

AMERICAN TWIST: A type of topspin serve used mainly in doubles play. The topspin imparts a high bounce allowing the server more time to follow the serve to the net.

APPROACH SHOT: The shot which is taken just before the hitter moves in to the net.

AUSTRALIAN DOUBLES: A formation in which the net person lines up on the same side as the server.

BACKCOURT: The court area between the service line and the baseline.

BASELINE: The backline or farthest line from the net.

BASELINE GAME: One who rarely attempts to take the net or play in the forecourt.

BIG GAME: A style of play popularized by Jack Kramer and utilizing the hard serve, followed by a pressing net attack.

CARRY: An illegal shot causing the ball to be slung or hit twice before crossing the net.

CENTER MARK: A short perpendicular line which divides the baseline at its center.

CHOP: A downward stroke of the racket, usually causing the ball to rise slightly and, depending on the surface, to skid or bounce low.

CLOSED TOURNAMENT: An event open only to the member of a particular club or geographical area.

CONTINENTAL GRIP: A grip utilizing a position halfway between an Eastern forehand and classic backhand. The grip does not require a player to change grips for the forehand and backhand stroke.

CROSS COURT SHOT: When the ball is hit diagonally from one side of the court to the opposite corner on the other side.

DEFAULT: When a match is awarded to one player because of non-appearance or if one player is unable to continue a match.

DEUCE: A 40-40 tie score and anytime thereafter in the same game when the score is even.

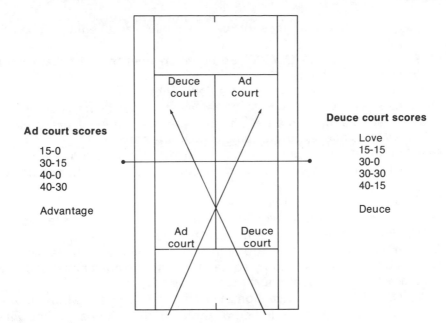

Ad court scores

15-0
30-15
40-0
40-30

Advantage

Deuce court scores

Love
15-15
30-0
30-30
40-15

Deuce

DEUCE COURT: The right service court viewed from one's own baseline.

DINK: A softly hit ball, usually intended to keep the ball in play.

DOUBLE FAULT: Failure to place either the first or second ball of one's serve into play.

DOUBLES: Match play between two teams of two players each. Mixed doubles involves having a male and female on each team.

DOWN THE LINE: A shot moving parallel to the sideline.

DROP SHOT: A lightly hit ball, usually having backspin, and designed to barely clear the net with minimum force.

EASTERN GRIP: Most used grip for hitting forehand shots. Also called the "shake hands grip."

FAST COURT: A smooth court surface causing the tennis ball to move quickly to the hitter.

FAULT: The failure to serve a ball within the proper service court.

FOOT FAULT: An illegal serve caused by the server stepping into the court as the racket makes contact with the ball.

GAME: One portion of a set which occurs when one person or team wins four points, and are at least two points ahead. On tie games, i.e. 30-30 or 40-40, it is the first side to gain a two-point lead.

GRAND SLAM: A tennis achievement requiring the winning of the U.S. Open, The French Open, The Australian Open, and Wimbledon all in the same year.

GROUND STROKE: A forehand or backhand stroke occurring after the ball has bounced.

HACKER: A tennis player with limited form and skills.

HALF VOLLEY: A defensive shot usually occurring when the ball is hit halfway between a volley and a regular ground stroke. The ball is blocked or hit with a very short backswing just as it begins to rise from a bounce.

INVITATIONAL TOURNAMENT: Competition open only to players who receive the invitation.

ILTF: The International Lawn Tennis Federation.

LET: Whenever a point needs to be replayed. Generally it occurs when a serve hits the top of the net and lands in the proper service area.

LET SERVE: As above, but pertains only to the service.

LOB: A high soft shot usually used to drive one's opponent back to the baseline, or to allow the hitter more time to assume better court position.

LOVE: Zero in tennis scoring.

MATCH: A tennis contest involving either singles, doubles or teams.

MATCH POINT: The final point needed to close out a match.

NET UMPIRE: When officials are employed, this person calls let serves.

NO OR OUT: The terms used by some players to denote a ball that did not land within the proper court area.

NO ADD SCORING: A new version of scoring requiring the winner to have four points. If the score is tied at three all, then the next point determines a winner.

NO MAN'S LAND: The court area located between the baseline and the service line. Generally considered to be a poor area to attack from or to defend.

OVERHEAD: A free swinging hard shot hit very much like the serve.

PASSING SHOT: A ball hit low and hard to the side of a person who has moved in to "take the net."

POACH: Generally refers to the doubles play of a net person who is able to pick off shots intended for a partner.

PRO SET: An abbreviated match which is completed when one player wins at least eight games and is ahead by at least two games.

PUSHER: A soft hitter who is generally very steady.

RALLY: An exchange of shots after the serve, usually from the baseline.

RECEIVER: The person who is to receive and return the serve.

RETRIEVER: A type of player who plays a defensive game and returns all shots.

SERVICE BREAK: The loss of a game by a server or a serving team.

SERVICE LINE: A line running parallel to and 21 feet from the net.

SET: A component part of a match which occurs when a player or side has won at least six games and is ahead by at least two games.

SLICE: To hit the ball with side spin and a slight undercutting motion.

SLOW COURT: A rough or soft surface court causing the tennis ball to "bite in" or to move more slowly to the hitter. Good examples of slow courts are clay and rubico (Har-tru).

SPLIT SETS: When both players or teams have won one set and the match outcome will be determined by the remaining set.

STRAIGHT SETS: To win a match without losing a set.

SUDDEN DEATH: When a tie breaker goes to the final point.

TAKE TWO: Whenever the receiver indicates that the server should repeat two serves.

USTA: An abbreviation for the United States Tennis Association.

VASS: An abbreviation for the Van Allen Simplified Scoring System. A set is completed whenever one person scores 21 or 31 points.

VIRGINIA SLIMS: A series of tournaments or regular competition for female tennis players who are professionals.

VOLLEY: A short backswing shot taken before the ball hits the court. It is the primary weapon for doubles play.

WESTERN GRIP: A forehand grip which allows the hitter to impart severe topspin to the ball.

WORLD TEAM TENNIS: An organization composed of the world's best male and female professional players.

CHAPTER 3 EVALUATION

1. Name the points you may win in a game, using the correct scoring terminology. Begin with the first point you can win and proceed progressively to the final point.

2. Abbreviated scoring terminology is frequently and universally used. What are the terms generally used?

3. You must win a minimum of_____points and be at least_____ahead to win a game.

4. The term "deuce" means that you and your opponent have each won at least_____points.

5. What is the definition of a set? How do you win a set using conventional scoring? Using a tiebreaker?

6. Explain how you win a match.

7. What is unique about the ninth point in the 9-point tiebreaker?

8. If a ball in play partially touches the line, is it a good shot?

9. When is a point won by a player? How can your opponent lose the point in play? Name several ways.

10. On the toss of the coin for service, you win. What are your choices?

11. When do my opponent and I change ends of the court?

12. The ball was clearly out of bounds when I caught it in mid-air. It had not touched the court yet. Whose point?

13. What is the ruling if you think a ball is out, but you are unsure, and there is no mark left by the ball?

14. Score this problem. A is serving, B is receiving.

POINT #	A	B	SCORE
1	X		
2	X		
3		X	
4	X		
5		X	
6		X	
7	X		
8		X	
9		X	
10		X	

CHAPTER 4

GRIPPING THE RACKET

HITTING THE TENNIS BALL

Since most of you have probably received elementary tennis instruction and have played some tennis prior to reading this book, you know that the forehand drive is the "bread and butter" shot of the game. It is quite likely that since this stroke seemed easier to hit than the backhand, you favored the shot, and now find yourself playing three quarters of the court with the forehand. You also may now pray that your opponent will not hit the ball down the line on the backhand side.

If this is the case, do not be unduly concerned since you must have a good forehand and the only way to acquire one is to practice hitting from that side. It does mean, however, that you must begin to hit a greater percentage of backhand shots, otherwise the difference in the ability to hit both shots will appreciate even more, and you will become more vulnerable.

As with any endeavor there are certain generalizations or "principles" which if applied will improve performance. This does not rule out individual differences. However, if one studies the current greats in tennis it will be quickly noted that most seem to have nearly identical form in their basic strokes.

FOREHAND GRIP

EASTERN

The Eastern Grip is the most commonly used grip of tennis players. It is often called the "shake hands" grip since the racket handle is grasped as you would the hand of a friend. The palm will be in the same plane as the face of the racket, and the heel of the hand will rest lightly against the butt of the handle. The fingers should be spread with the index finger spread slightly more than the others. This will cause a "V" (the junction of the thumb and index finger) to rest squarely on top of the handle so that if a line were to be drawn from the "V" it would fall over the right shoulder.

EASTERN FOREHAND GRIP

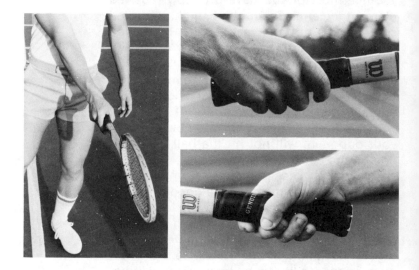

CONTINENTAL GRIP

The Continental is a grip that places the hand midway between the Eastern forehand and the Eastern backhand. The advantage is that "no change has to be made for forehand or backhand shots." Thus, this grip is sometimes favored by players who react slowly at the net, by players who volley a great deal, and by players who play doubles exclusively.

The disadvantage is a slight reduction in hitting power, and the necessity of a strong wrist. To assume the Continental grip move your hand around the handle to the left of the Eastern grip. The knuckle of your index finger will rest halfway between the top of the handle (as the classic backhand) and the back of the handle (as the Eastern forehand). Finger

CONTINENTAL GRIP

Side View

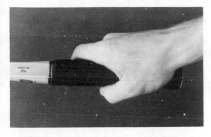

Top View

spread and thumb position is the same as the Eastern forehand. See Continental picture.

WESTERN

The Western Grip is achieved by moving the hand in a clockwise direction from the Eastern grip, or hand shaking grip, so that the palm of the hand will be more under the handle rather than behind it as in the Eastern.

Although this grip does permit exaggerated topspin to be placed on the ball it is not practical since the hand must be moved a greater distance to hit the backhand stroke, and in a fast exchange there is simply not enough time. The Western grip is rarely used by top notch players and is not recommended for beginners by the authors.

WESTERN GRIP

Rear View

Front View

MOST COMMON ERRORS OF THE FOREHAND GRIP

1. *The fingers are too close together resulting in a hammer grip.*
2. *The player grips the racket too tightly in between shots resulting in a hammer grip.*
2. *The player grips the racket too tightly in between shots resulting in muscle fatigue.*
3. *The grip is not firm enough at impact.*
4. *The index finger is not wrapped around the handle but rather points toward the head of the racket.*
5. *Improper angle of the wrist.*

THE EASTERN BACKHAND

One of the most common faults among beginners is the attempt to hit backhand shots without turning the racket. Unless the racket is turned it will be impossible to present the racket face perpendicularly to the ball and at the same time maintain a smooth fluid stroke. To place the racket face in the desired position you must turn the hand a quarter turn counterwise from the Eastern forehand grip. This will place the knuckle of your index finger **on top of the handle.** The thumb should be kept at a diagonal, but may be shifted upward slightly for additional support. The fingers should be spread slightly as in the Eastern forehand. For best results, turn the racket by simultaneously loosening the forehand grip and turning the throat of the racket with the left thumb and index finger. This should be done as the left hand is guiding the racket back into a full backswing.

EASTERN BACKHAND GRIPS

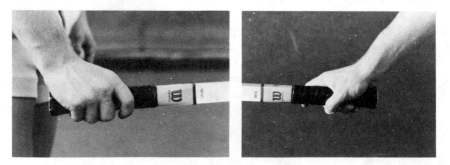

MOST COMMON ERRORS OF THE BACK-HAND GRIP

1. *Failure to change from the forehand grip.*
2. *Improper placement of the thumb or forefinger.*
3. *Insecure grip at moment of impact.*

THE TWO-HANDED BACKHAND

In the last several years a number of ranking tennis players have demonstrated that the two-hand backhand can be a very effective weapon. Its advantage lies in allowing a person to hit with more power, in controlling the racket more effectively if the person is very small or weak, and providing a better opportunity to hit with topspin. Its chief disadvantage is that one can not reach as far on wide shots as with the conventional backhand. To assume the two-handed backhand grip, place your right hand in the same position as for the Eastern backhand. The left hand is placed in a position similar to the Eastern forehand, but just above and touching the right hand. Both hands should be placed on the grip at the beginning of the pivot turn and preparatory to the backswing.

The right hand plays the dominant role with the left providing added wrist support, control, and power. Contact with the ball should occur as the ball reaches the front foot. Extremely wide shots may necessitate your releasing the racket with your left hand as you hit. See two-hand backhand pictures.

TWO-HANDED BACKHAND GRIPS

Using right backhand, left forehand

Using 2 forehand grips

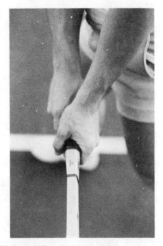

Using right backhand, left forehand

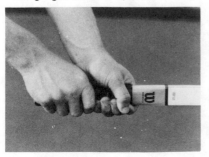

Using 2 forehand grips

CHAPTER 4 EVALUATION

1. Contrast the Eastern, Western, and Continental grips.

2. List some of the more common errors associated with the Eastern forehand grip.

3. What are some of the more common errors associated with the Eastern Backhand grip?

4. What are the advantages of the two-hand backhand vs the conventional backhand grip?

5. Why should the tennis stroke and serve exclude superfluous movement?

6. What is the relationship between ball spin and ball speed?

CHAPTER 5

PRINCIPLES OF STROKING

SIMPLICITY

Most of you I am sure have heard the story of the man who was to deliver an important speech and how his wife, who while typing the speech, made a notation at the top of the page. The notation was in the form of the four letters KISS with an arrow drawn to the bottom of the page. At the bottom of the page were the words "Keep it simple, stupid."

So the first principle of hitting the tennis ball is to "keep the stroke simple." The writer once knew a fairly good player who swung at a tennis ball and hit himself in the mouth with his own tennis racket. The end result was eight stitches. Obviously he had not read this book and his stroke was not a simple stroke. The tennis swing is not a complicated windup with fancy gyrations as is sometimes seen. Rather it is a smooth, nearly effortless, and fluid motion which causes the head of the racket to increase momentum culminating on impact so that the total power of the swing is transferred into the tennis ball. One way to help develop this fluid swing is to stand in front of a mirror and simply "dry swing" your tennis racket while thinking of the various components that go to make up a good stroke.

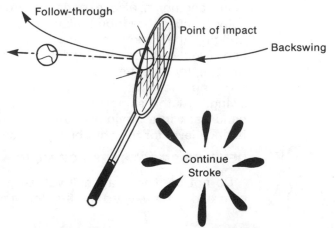

Follow-through

Point of impact

Backswing

Continue Stroke

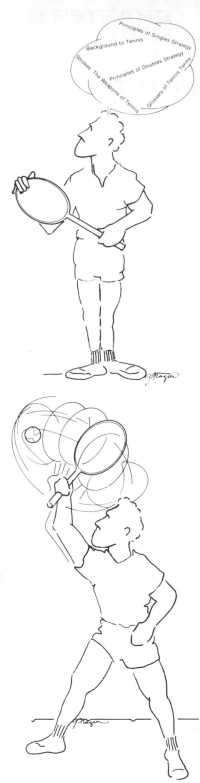

CONCENTRATION

It is quite probable that this principle, more than any other, separates the winners from the losers in tennis. When hitting the tennis ball you must drive all thoughts from your mind and concentrate almost entirely on watching the tennis ball. The vast majority of missed shots in tennis are due to the person making the shot not totally watching the ball. The principle also applies to other sports. Ted Williams, the famous baseball hitter, is attributed to having said that he always tried to follow the baseball with his eyes from the pitcher's hand to the moment of impact with his bat. One way to assist in the development of stroke concentration is to never look up until after you have hit the tennis ball. How often have you looked to see what your opponent was doing just as you were about to hit the ball?

ELIMINATE UNNECESSARY MOTION

If you attempt to hit a moving target with a rifle or pistol while you are moving you will probably experience great difficulty. However, if you stop or hesitate, even momentarily, you would notice a great improvement in accuracy. The identical is true in tennis. Beginning tennis players will find great improvement in stroking ability if they cease moving just prior to hitting the ball. Another problem frequently experienced by beginners is an unnecessary bending motion at the knees and hips, so that in addition to unnecessary lateral motion they also are bobbing up and down with the stroke. Many beginners also experience great difficulty because they loop their swing instead of bringing the racket back more in a straight line. If you are experiencing difficulty in hitting the ball, try repeating to yourself just prior to stroking the shot, "Straight back — step swing." At the same time, bring the racket hand back in a straight line at the expected bounce level for the shot being played.

DEVELOP SMOOTHNESS OF MOTION

Do not be discouraged if you seem to appear and feel awkward the first few times you attempt a new stroke or new movement. Try to remember your first attempt at riding a bicycle. Repetition will increase your smoothness and ultimately your movements will become as "smooth as silk."

CONTROL

As a beginner your primary goal should be consistency and accuracy rather than speed or spin. To develop the "feel or touch" necessary for consistency you should concentrate on hitting the ball with only moderate pace. In time you will gain confidence in your strokes, and will want to gradually increase the pace of your shots.

Spin is imparted to the tennis ball by the angle of the racket face at the moment of impact. The basic spin is a slight topspin created by starting the shot low and finishing high thus causing the ball to spin from top to bottom and resulting in a downward drop or curve in the flight of the ball.

BALANCE AND POWER

Balance is fundamental to all sports and tennis is not an exception. The ability to handle low shots and to move quickly in any direction necessitates that you be relaxed and with the knees slightly flexed. Power is the force that is gained by the fine coordination of racket, arm, and weight transfer necessary to move the ball in the direction you wish it to go. Early preparation is essential. Just as in softball where the batter steps into the pitch, you should step into the line of shot. This is accomplished by transferring your body weight to the forward stepping foot which is kept flat on the ground. The heel of the back foot is usually off the ground and bears little weight. The face of the racket then moves into and through the intended flight path of the ball. Additional power and a free swing will be possible if you are able to keep your waist relatively straight. However, remember that an increase in power can contribute to loss of control. So proceed with caution.

CHAPTER 5 EVALUATION

1. Which stroke principle is the most important insofar as being the determining factor in winning or losing?

2. Most stroke errors are caused by a simple, easy to correct technique. What is it?

3. Why is it desirable to cease your movement pattern just prior to executing your tennis stroke?

4. How would you rank the following words — spin, power, speed, control, and accuracy? Explain why your ranking has been put in this order.

5. As a beginner, you should be primarily concerned with one characteristic. What is it?

6. The basic stroking technique will impart which type of spin on the ball.

7. An increase of power into the stroke can cause another problem. Name the problem.

8. How would you describe the simplicity of a tennis stroke? Begin from the ready position.

CHAPTER 6

FOOTWORK — BASIC PATTERNS

As a beginner, intermediate or advanced player, you soon realize that each stroke, whether it be a forehand or backhand, is very similar to the one preceding. The only difference is that the strokes may be made in different places. Hence the importance of footwork. It is most desirable to be able to move fluently and in a relaxed, controlled manner. Of all the ingredients of developing a successful and satisfying level of tennis, footwork is one of the most important. It has been said that footwork is 50 to 70 percent of the game. While this may be debatable, it certainly is a vital area that cannot be overlooked or taken lightly. As you observe a good player, you can easily see the relationship of footwork to stroke production and success.

Many inexperienced players appear to hit the ball in all sorts of positions. Most of these are uncomfortable, and the results are frequently unsatisfactory. Good footwork makes a difficult job easy. As stated earlier, most strokes follow the same basic technique — forehands are stroked about the same way each time, with slight adjustments. Backhands, volleys, etc., are the same. The difference in forehands may frequently be in footwork preparation. The following explanations of proper footwork patterns will progress from the simple to the complex.

THE READY POSITION

As a player begins to learn the game of tennis, he or she soon realizes that tennis balls cross the net at various speeds, angles and heights. It is infrequent that two shots in a row are the same. Thus, there is an immediate

The ready position

need to be continuously prepared, expecting everything. You may find yourself having to move quickly in any direction, covering half the court either on the forehand side or the backhand side. On the other hand you may have to move very little, except to step forward and contact the ball. Alertness is the key!

The ready position is the stance used to facilitate quick movements. That is to say, the player can move in any direction, quickly and totally under control, whether the move is one step or a series of steps.

In describing the ready position, we find the body situated in the following manner. The racket is held comfortably, usually with an Eastern forehand grip. The other hand supports the racket, holding it loosely at the throat. The arms are usually close in to the body, supporting the racket at a position comfortably in front of the upper torso. The elbows are relatively close to the chest. The waist is slightly bent, allowing the body to bend forward comfortably indicating a position of readiness. The knees are slightly flexed, with the weight evenly distributed on the balls of the feet. The feet are spread about a shoulder width apart. The keynote is comfort. In advanced tennis, it is not unusual to see the player receiving service jump slightly upon anticipating the contact of the ball on the server's racket. In fact, it probably happens more times than not.

THE FORWARD PIVOT

For balls close to the body — one step away.

Actually this footwork pattern may be done in three different ways, each correct and proper in its own style. Each style accomplishes the procedure of turning the body sideways to the net, allowing the racket to proceed into the backswing, and if completed properly, stepping into the stroke, thereby creating a weight shift into the flow of the stroke. The three variations are explained below.

The cross step pivot. This variation begins with the ready position. As the ball approaches the player, the player pivots on the

THE TURN and STEP PIVOT. *Left to right:* Ready position; Turn feet to side; Step and stroke.

ball of the right foot and steps across and slightly forward with the left foot. As the ball approaches the contact area, a slight weight shift is made as the racket moves into the ball. Upon the completion of the stroke, the weight is on the forward foot. The rear foot remains stationary. The toes are in contact with the ground, but the heel will be slightly raised.

This footwork pattern will remain the same for both the forehand and the backhand stroke.

The turn and step pivot. This variation involves two separate movements by the player. As the ball approaches, the player merely turns the body to the side. There is no distinct footwork pattern, but a cross step may be used as discussed above. However, the forward foot will line up with the rear foot in a position approximately parallel to the net. The feet are kept close together. As the ball approaches, the player steps into the ball at a 45 degree angle, shifting the weight into the stroke as contact is made. The follow-through remains the same as in the crossover pivot.

The twist and step pivot. The third variation is similar, yet quite different from the other pivot procedures. In this method the player, upon seeing the ball approach, simply turns sideways to the net, pivoting the feet to the side from the ready position. As the ball approaches, the foot closer to the net steps at a 45 degree angle into the ball as the forward swing is initiated.

The follow-through for this pivot, as in the others listed above, remains the same. The weight is forward at the completion of the stroke. In all three variations the recovery to the ready position simply involves stepping back with the forward foot, again facing the net, and resuming the ready position.

These three footwork patterns will include many variations among players. Basically, however, the user will find that these three variations will more than suffice for stroking forehands and backhands with proper form. It should be noted that these same patterns are used with the backhand.

THE REVERSE PIVOT

The reverse pivot is used when the ball is coming either directly to the body or so close to the hitter that using a forward pivot would crowd the stroke. In order to properly position oneself for this stroke, the reverse pivot is used starting with the basic ready position as shown. The following pattern is used for the right handed hitter.

With the feet in the ready position, begin your initial movement by a slight crouching movement in the knees. This is started as soon as the flight of the ball is determined. With the weight evenly distributed on the balls of both feet, simply pivot on the left foot and step to the rear with the right foot, turning the body to face the forehand side as you step. Position the feet as shown in the illustration. Having positioned yourself thusly, put your weight once again on the right (rear) foot. You are

THE REVERSE PIVOT

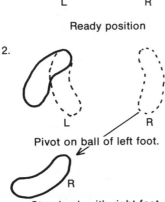

1.

L   R

Ready position

2.

L   R

Pivot on ball of left foot.

R

Step back with right foot.

now in a position very similar to those mentioned earlier under the forehand pivot.

As the ball approaches the contact area, with the weight comfortably on the rear foot, execute a forward step into the ball, as was done with the basic forward pivot. Very simply explained, you have just stepped back and away from a ball coming in too close to the body, and have placed yourself in a position so you can comfortably reach the ball and execute the stroke.

The reverse pivot is identical for the forehand and the backhand. The player will receive much benefit by starting early in preparing for the stroke.

THE SIDE-SKIP OR SHUFFLE STEP

This footwork pattern is used when the ball is away from the body — not close enough to be reached by a simple forward pivot. The side-skip pattern is a comfortable, easy movement that allows the body to pivot into the ball without breaking the flowing, rhythmical motion.

As with the other footwork patterns, the starting position is the ready position. As the ball is hit by the opponent, the footwork pattern should begin. This promptness is necessary because of the distance one must travel to get into position, and is complicated by the speed, depth and spin of the ball.

When moving to the right side, the first step is with the right foot. Initially, a slight crouch is taken by the player, and the weight is moved by pushing with the ball of the left foot, and stepping with the right foot to the side. The step should cover about three feet, or a distance that is comfortable for the player. When the right foot comes in contact with the court, the left foot follows and comes into place along side, thus completing the first "step" of the side-skip pattern.

This pattern continues until the player is one skip or step away from the desirable pivot point. As the final step is made, the player begins a forward pivot into the ball, as

Ready position

Series showing side skip

explained earlier in the chapter. That is to say, on the last step, the right foot contacts the court and a pivot is made, pointing the right toe at a 45 degree angle to the net. As the weight is taken on the right foot, the left foot begins the step-across into the ball, continuing the 45 degree angle mentioned above. As the stroke is made, the weight will be maintained in the pattern outlined and no additional steps will be needed, except to recover into a ready position. However, this movement pattern is used to take the player away from the "home" position on the court, usually to the corners. It will be necessary to use it again to recover back to the center of the baseline (backcourt) area for the next stroke.

method of footwork patterns   Completed stroke

In moving to a ball that is either short in the court or to one that is deep, pushing you back away from the baseline, a short sidestep motion is used, very similar to the step illustrated above. Short, quick steps are used rather than longer ones, as some adjustment will be necessary due to the low or high bounce. A player can greatly improve the situation by maintaining an alert, intense attitude. This will create a quicker initial response to each shot.

Finally, it should be noted that every player must frequently "run" to reach the ball. This happens when the player is too far from the ball and cannot otherwise reach the shot. However, upon reaching the ball, proper adjustments are necessary to create proper stroke footwork.

TIPS ON FOOTWORK

1. Keep a close watch on the ball to insure an early "jump" on the incoming shot. Begin your preparation as soon as the ball leaves the opponent's racket.
2. Anticipate where your opponent will hit each shot and begin moving early.
3. Look at the possible angles of return — to your right and left — now recover to the center of this angle.
4. When you contact the ball and return it to your opponent, recover quickly, as soon as your follow-through is completed.
5. In order to gain maximum benefit from your footwork pattern, your movement into the stroke should be rhythmical, relaxed, comfortable and EARLY.
6. Be in position with racket cocked in the backswing EARLY — this means no later than the bounce of the incoming ball.
7. As you execute your stroke, keep the rear foot IN PLACE only allowing the weight to shift forward to the other foot. DO NOT STEP with the rear foot as the stroke is made.

CHAPTER 6 EVALUATION

1. Describe the ready position.

2. Demonstrate the following: Cross Step Pivot, Turn and Step Pivot, Reverse Pivot and Side-Skip.

3. List 5 footwork tips.

4. Most receivers move slightly as the server contacts the ball. Why is this?

5. What grip is used when in the ready position? Why?

6. What is the purpose of the reverse pivot?

7. What part does good footwork play in the game of tennis?

8. Ideally, where should you strive to contact the ball?

9. What is anticipation? How can it assist you?

10. Which footwork pattern is used most to move from side to side in the backcourt area?

CHAPTER 7

THE FOREHAND

HITTING THE FOREHAND

Since we have previously discussed the Eastern grip and ready position we are now ready to proceed to a discussion of stroking fundamentals for the forehand drive.

BACKSWING

The backswing is started as soon as you see that the ball will land on the forehand side. Beginners will experience more success by drawing the racket back in a straight line until the head of the racket is pointing directly at the fence behind the baseline. This is accomplished by turning the left shoulder and moving toward the ball so that when the ball arrives your early backswing will allow you time to adjust to unusual spin, speed, or a bad bounce. As you acquire more experience you will probably find yourself looping the racket head slightly in the form of an egg-shaped half arc.

At the point of full backswing the racket head should be just slightly below the point at which you will hit the ball. This provides a low to high swing which is necessary for imparting slight topspin to the ball. For low bouncing shots you must bend the knees and drop the shoulder farthest from the net. This will prevent the head of the racket from dropping below the handle and is very necessary for maintaining control.

PIVOT AND MOVEMENT OF FEET

Your beginning position should be with the feet approximately shoulder width, in the center of the court, and one to three feet behind the base line. As you move to the ball and stop at the desired position, your weight

THE FOREHAND STROKE

Backswing: Rear view (left) and side view (right)

Contact point   Follow-through

should be on the rear foot. The next movement is a step into the ball, much as a softball hitter does when stepping into a pitch. This transfers your weight into the line of shot and provides the power necessary for a successful stroke. Additional points of importance are:

1. Stand straight from the waist up.
2. The front knee should never be stiff.
3. The toe of your back foot will be in contact with the ground but the heel will be off the ground.

IMPACT POINT

Whenever possible, you should hit the ball at waist level since this is the easiest and most effective point of impact. Should the ball be lower than waist level, lower the racket arm by bending the knees and not the back.

As your weight transfers to the front foot and the racket head moves toward the impact point, you should attempt to make contact with the ball slightly in advance of the front foot and beyond the midpoint of your body.

Follow-through is as important to tennis as it is to basketball shooting, throwing a football, or any other athletic endeavor involving hand-eye coordination. Perhaps the easiest way to develop follow-through is to establish checkpoints in your swing which, if adhered to, will guarantee that follow-through is taking place.

Follow-through checkpoints:

1. At the completion of your forward swing, is your front knee slightly bent with the ball of your foot in contact with the court?
2. Is the heel of your other foot (the back leg) slightly off the court at the conclusion of the swing?
3. Did you start the backswing low and finish in a high position — well out in front of your body and at least eye high?
4. Are you standing tall from the waist at the end of your follow-through?
5. Is the racket face still standing on edge at the end of your forward swing?
6. At the completion of your swing, are you looking over your elbow and forearm to where you want the ball to go?

When hitting the forehand, always try to think of the racket as being an extension of your arm. You are trying to use your arm and racket much as you would if you were trying to sweep a full table of dishes onto the floor in one full sweeping motion.

Remember to relax your grip between shots. Otherwise the muscles of your arm, hand, and wrist will experience early fatigue.

MOST COMMON FOREHAND ERRORS

Do you often hit the ball long? If you are consistently hitting balls long it may be because your opponent is hitting the ball hard. Do not try to hit with a slugger. Use his speed by shortening your backswing and letting the ball ricochet off your racket. Another possibility is that the face of your racket is open or tilted too far up. Or you may be allowing the ball to descend too far on the bounce before hitting. Try to take the ball at its highest point of bounce and bring the racket head back on a higher plane.

Do you often hit short or hit weak shots? The lack of hitting power usually results whenever you do not step into the ball and do not shift your weight with each shot. Are you following through on each shot and does the racket head finish well in front of the body? You may be delaying your swing and allowing the ball to get past you. Move your impact point forward. Late hits are sometimes caused because you do not begin the backswing soon enough.

Do you consistently hit shots to the right (right handers) or to the left (left handers)? It is likely that either your feet are lined up improperly or you are swinging late. Practice hurrying the backswing and try to move your impact point in front of the midpoint of your body.

Are you hitting the ball consistently to the left or "pulling the ball"? In this case you may be hitting too soon or you may not have your feet lined up properly.

Does the ball always seem to land right at your feet? The old axiom is "all the way up or all the way back, but not in between." The area in between the back service line and the base line is called "No Man's Land" and is a poor place to be caught.

Are you spraying shots? Do they just go in all directions with no set pattern? Try setting up more quickly. This means "hustle." Other problems are looking at your opponent instead of the ball and hitting with a "loose wrist." Try to maintain a firm wrist and do not try to hit either a racketball, table tennis, or badminton shot. Good tennis requires a wrist that is a little more firm than any of the other mentioned sports.

CHAPTER 7 EVALUATION

1. What is the reason for the grip on the forehand stroke? Point out the differences in hand positions and the resulting changes in stroke technique as compared to the backhand.

2. How soon should you begin your footwork preparation for the forehand stroke? Where will you want to hit the ball (contact point) in reference to your body if you have a choice?

3. Name the three grips recommended for use in the forehand stroke. How do they differ?

4. The vast majority of players will use the Eastern forehand grip. What are the advantages of using this grip compared to the others?

5. What is your "home position"?

6. List and explain the three basic parts of the forehand stroke.

7. What is the importance of the follow-through? What purpose does it serve?

8. At the completion of the stroke, where are the feet placed and how is the weight distributed?

9. What corrections would you make if you are consistently hitting the ball long? Why is this problem caused?

10. Why will you need to lay the wrist back in your backswing when executing a forehand stroke?

11. What is the problem when you are consistently stroking the ball to the right side of the court out of bounds?

12. At which height should the racket be taken in the backswing? Describe the path of the racket coming into the ball.

13. Where is "No Man's Land"? Explain the problems of playing here.

CHAPTER 8

THE BACKHAND

To many people, the backhand is the most difficult stroke in tennis. To others, it is their strongest stroke. The difference probably is in the dedication and determination of the player to properly learn the fundamentals of the backhand, and then to practice enough to groove the shot.

Due to a necessary grip change, the backhand sometimes feels insecure, and it is easily understood that a sense of weakness might occur. Understanding the proper technique of the stroke will overcome most of these fears, and provision of enough practice time will generate sufficient confidence in the backhand.

CHANGING THE GRIP

The Eastern forehand grip, used by the vast majority of players, is the most comfortable grip known in tennis. It is easy to understand why it is so popular. The "shake hands" grip is easy to obtain, comfortable to hold, and blends well with the physics of technique. However, it is not a proper grip for the backhand. This is due primarily to the required change in the angle of the face of the racket.

The grip change from the Eastern forehand to the Eastern backhand simply involves a rotation of the hand one quarter turn counterclockwise to the left on the handle. This will make the following checkpoints:

    a. The racket face will become flat, allowing more hitting area for the ball.

    b. The "V" formed by the thumb and forefinger will be on the top of the left bevel on the handle.

THE BACKHAND STROKE

Backswing   Forward   Contact   Follow-through
approach

c. The large knuckle of the forefinger will be atop the top forward bevel of the handle.

d. The fingers will remain spread to allow more control along the entire racket handle.

e. The palm of the hand, if opened, will face down toward the ground.

f. The thumb will comfortably lie alongside the handle, diagonally across the rear facet — not with the "thumbprint" on the facet.

It should be emphasized that *wrist action be kept to an absolute minimum.* The less wrist the better.

Although this grip will be less comfortable initially to the player, constant use will generate a positive attitude toward the change, and a vast improvement in the game.

The change from forehand grip to backhand grip usually occurs as the ball is travelling toward the player. Most players, in the ready position, will use a forehand grip while waiting for the ball. As the ball approaches toward the backhand, however, the change becomes necessary. While moving the body for proper stroke alignment, simply change from forehand to backhand grip, supporting the racket with the other hand at the throat.

THE BACKSWING

As the ball approaches, the body is moving into position using proper footwork procedures. When the body begins to turn to the side, the grip change should be completed. Usually a player will keep both hands on the racket — one on the handle, and one supporting the racket along the throat during the backswing.

Ideally, the ball should be timed so that it is struck at a level between the knee and the waist — in the general area of the hip or thigh. Therefore, the backswing should be taken back at the same height as the anticipated contact point — hip high. As the racket is taken back, the racket arm tends to straighten, allowing the handle to stay down at the level of contact. That is, the racket hand is down below the waist. The support arm, along the throat of the handle, is also kept relatively straight. This causes the racket to remain parallel to the ground throughout the backswing, and the face of the racket perpendicular to the court.

The length of the backswing will differ depending on the speed of the incoming ball, and the quickness of the player. Usually a full backswing is desirable, taking the racket back just past a line of 180 degrees or perpendicular to the net.

The wrist is kept firm throughout the entire backswing procedure and the grip is kept tight along the handle of the racket. Caution should be used to maintain a LEVEL backswing. The player should not lift the racket head or drop it downward as the initial backswing movement is started. An important reminder is that the racket should be taken back on a plane level with the anticipated contact area. Remember that the ball will come at various heights, causing some backswing movements on a low level and others at a high level. Fortunately, most are in the center of the extremes. The basic keys to success are (1) watching the ball closely and (2) getting an early start in your backswing preparation.

THE CONTACT AREA

When hitting a ball using the backhand stroke, we must remember that the ball contacts the racket six to eight inches in front of the forward foot. That is to say, the racket is further "toward the net" than in the forehand.

As the ball approaches, the racket begins its forward motion toward the ball. The hand tightens on the racket handle and the arm becomes more firm as the forward motion of the racket continues. It is necessary to make the wrist as strong as possible to absorb the impact of the ball. An important criteria for a successful stroke is to be certain that the head flow of the racket leads the way into the ball. In other words, it does not trail the wrist and arm action moving forward. Rather, the arm, wrist and racket flow as one smooth pattern in a straight path. The major strength for the movement pattern is from the shoulder.

A major effort should be made by the player to keep the shoulders level with the court throughout the entire stroke. This will eliminate the common error of raising the shoulder of the racket arm on contact, causing the ball to fly on an upward trajectory and frequently going out of bounds.

As the motion flows from the backswing into contact of the ball, a strong effort should be made to keep the stroke in a level "parallel to the court" pattern. The level path of the racket will allow maximum head contact with the ball, providing a drive that goes relatively deep into the opponent's court, and will create a slight amount of topspin to bring the ball down on the court.

Since the contact point is being made six to eight inches in front of the body, maximum use can be made of the forward shift of weight into the ball. However, care must be observed to keep from lifting the ball. As the racket meets the ball, the hitter should drive through the ball to establish a definite drive pattern — usually four inches to six inches will suffice.

THE FOLLOW-THROUGH

The follow-through is in reality the guidance system for the stroke. For example, if the follow-through is low, the ball will stay low. If it is straight, the ball does not clear the net, but usually will hit near the net cord.

Proper follow-through begins at the conclusion of the contact with the ball, and is a smooth, upward flow of the racket. Please note that sufficient upward movement should be started while the ball is still on the racket strings, or the follow-through is to no avail. Simply stated, the follow-through lifts the ball over the net in the direction aimed by the racket.

The desired direction of the ball is determined from the direction of the racket head after contact. If the desired flight is crosscourt then the upward movement of the racket head is crosscourt. If you desire the ball to go down the line, then the upward motion is down the line, etc. This is the basic pattern for aiming the ball — and it works.

The player should note that the wrist is kept firm throughout the follow-through, and the racket arm is kept straight in order to give proper guidance to the ball. This will greatly aid in controlling the stroke.

THE TWO-HANDED STROKE

This is probably the latest innovation in tennis. Although it is not new, the two-handed stroke has recently become very popular. This is possibly due to the fantastic successes of some of the world's leading players such as Chris Evert, Jimmy Connors, and Harold Solomon. This trend is not without some justification, however. For example, a youngster just learning the game at age ten will definitely find strength a problem in using one hand for the backhand. At early stages of development, the wrist, grip, and arm are not strong enough to adequately control the racket upon impact with the ball, thus the two-handed stroke becomes a means to a successful end.

TWO-HANDED BACKSTROKE

| Backswing | Contact (front) | Contact (side) | Follow-through |

Although there are reach limitations in this stroke, proper footwork will overcome the problem. The user of the two-handed stroke should be very conscious of developing proper footwork patterns and the necessity of using them for each stroke. There is no substitute for good footwork.

Which grip(s) to use is sometimes a complex question. However, there is a relatively simple answer. The hitter has two choices.

1. The normal racket hand will use a correct *Eastern backhand* grip, and the support hand will compliment this using an Eastern *forehand* grip. See page 39.
2. Use two Eastern forehand grips.

The player may experiment with either of these two; however, the authors feel that the grip illustrated in #1 above is the most comfortable. Support for this stems from the idea that if the learner is young, and strength is developed, there will possibly be a tendency to move to a one-hand stroke. In such case, the proper grip will have been learned.

Basic techniques for the stroke will follow the normal pattern explained earlier. It should be noted that to achieve satisfaction in consistency, accuracy and pace, early preparation and proper footwork, combined with the appropriate backswing, level stroke, and fluid follow-through, are essential. Dedicated practice will be the primary keynote to success.

TIPS ON TECHNIQUE FOR
THE BACKHAND

1. Get ready early with proper foot-work and backswing.
2. Keep your eye on the ball.
3. Turn the right side toward the net.
4. Change your grip as you pivot.
5. Take the racket back waist high.
6. Keep the racket arm relatively straight.
7. Step into the ball with the right foot as you stroke.
8. Contact the ball in front of the right side.
9. Lead with the head of the racket.
10. As you stroke, be relaxed as you swing.
11. Keep your stroke **level** until the follow-through.
12. Stroke through the ball and up in the follow-through.

COMMON ERRORS AND HOW TO CORRECT THEM

Contacting the ball late — behind the forward foot. Begin your preparation earlier, as soon as the ball leaves the racket of your opponent. Watch the ball closely — anticipate the probable direction of the ball. Have racket back at full backswing position by the time the ball bounces.

Too much wrist used. As the pivot is made, tighten the grip on the handle, straighten the arm, and strengthen the wrist. Begin forward movement early, leading with the racket head. This is done by turning the entire arm into the stroke.

Leading with the wrist or elbow. This common error is corrected by mentally preparing early for the stroke, and concentrating on allowing the racket head to lead the way into the hit. Stroking with the shoulder and weight shift rather than just an arm and wrist movement. Keep the arm, wrist, hand and racket in a straight line as the stroke is made.

Trajectory is too low. Follow-through is low, or begins too late. As soon as hit is made in front of the body bring the racket head up sharply into the desired direction.

Trajectory is too high. Too much wrist used in the stroke, thereby accelerating the racket head as contact is made or the ball is hit, the shoulder is lifted upward, causing the flight of the ball to angle up. A high trajectory can also be caused by opening the face of the racket as contact is made. Correction is made by flattening the face of the racket somewhat.

Too much topspin. Improper face on the racket (closed) at contact, or the trajectory of the forward movement of the racket into the hit is improper. This is usually caused by either dropping the racket head initially or swinging upward at a sharp angle into the ball. Wrist becomes a problem here also. Level out the stroke, as explained earlier, and correct the racket face.

Ball pulls to the right (crosscourt) excessively. Caused primarily by poor footwork. Adjust stance and timing. Contact ball six to eight inches in front of body. Allow follow-through to only extend in the desired direction.

SKILLS PROGRESSIONS FOR FOREHAND AND BACKHAND

DRILLS   REPETITIONS

1. From a ready position, obtain the correct grip. Release. Repeat.   5
2. From a ready position try the forward pivot, check foot position, recover.   10
3. Repeat No. 2 above using the reverse pivot.   10
4. Using the forward pivot, take the complete backswing. Check the height of the racket head.   10
5. Using the forward pivot, combine the backswing, forward swing, and the follow-through in one smooth motion.   10
6. From the back of the court, drop a ball in front of the desired side and stroke the ball into the fence 20 feet away. Recover to the ready position. Repeat.   25
7. Have a partner toss from the net (center) to the center line. Stroke using full pivot.   30
8. Toss from net into the backcourt area (use a target) and stroke from the baseline into the opponent's court. Use full pivot.   30
9. Tosser will bounce and stroke a ball from the service line to partner at baseline on opposite side of the net. Pivot and stroke the ball back toward the tosser.   50
10. Hitter either drops ball or hits tossed ball into target area. (See diagram for accuracy drill.)

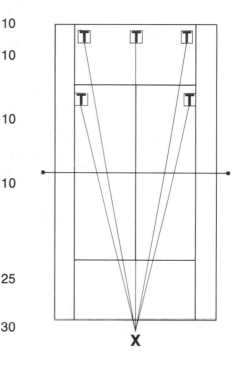

IF A REBOUND WALL IS AVAILABLE

11. Drop a ball as in #6 and stroke it to a rebound wall. Catch the ball, drop and repeat.   25
12. Repeat #10, keeping the ball to the right half of the forward rebound wall. The net line should be observed.   20
13. Repeat #11, keeping the ball to the left half of the forward rebound wall. Observe the net line.   20
14. Try to replay the rebound against the forward wall. (Number of bounces is not important at this stage.)   30
15. Drop a ball and stroke to your partner on the opposite side of the net. Try to continue as a rally.   30 min.

CHAPTER 8 EVALUATION

1. Describe the change from the Eastern forehand grip to the Eastern backhand.

2. Discuss the check points of an Eastern backhand swing, i.e., backswing, contact point, and follow-through.

3. Discuss three common errors of the backhand stroke and give directions for their remedy.

4. Diagram five drills suited to the development of a strong backhand.

CHAPTER 9

THE SERVE

Maurice McLaughlin set the tennis world on its ear in 1912 with a blistering serve that eventually won him the coveted U.S. Championship. Since that time other tennis greats such as Ellsworth Vines, Jack Kramer, Pancho Gonzales, and Roscoe Tanner have decisively demonstrated that a tennis ball can be hit at speeds upward of 110 miles per hour and that the serve is the primary weapon of attack.

Most professionals feel that more than half of all match points are won or lost as a direct result of the serve. They also feel that a true champion must "hold service" as a first prerequisite in any march to a tournament victory. Obviously if this is true for the advanced player then it is equally if not more important to success for the beginning and intermediate player.

THE SLICE SERVE

As indicated previously the slice serve is very important to all tennis players. Since the ball has both side spin and underspin it is very difficult for an opponent to return this serve with excessive speed or precision. Hence, it is heavily relied upon as a second serve when the ball must be placed in play.

To hit the serve place the racket grip in a Continental position (halfway between forehand and backhand). Your front foot should be at a 45 degree angle and approximately 2-3 feet from the center mark.

STANCE

Your initial position for serving (in singles play) should be a position two to four feet from the center mark. This permits you to bisect the angle of the return of serve thus equalizing the distance required to move for your return. Your feet and body should be in a throwing or hitting stance with the front toe at a 45 degree angle, about two inches behind the service line, and on a line parallel to the intended path of the ball. One necessary adjustment is to shift your toes so they are pointing at the right net post. Advanced players sometimes prefer to have both feet more parallel to the service line since this affords greater opportunity to uncoil the hips as the ball is being hit. If you continue to serve the ball too far to the left from this position even after adjusting your aim and wrist movement, you may need to move your rear foot slightly back and to the rear of the front foot. This will place your nonhitting shoulder more sideways to the net and should move the ball to the right.

Your stance should be reasonably wide, at least shoulder width since this allows you to shift your weight to the back foot on the backswing and to the front foot during contact with the ball. As the toss is made the rear foot should slide forward allowing a little more racket on impact with the ball.

At moment of impact the body should have enough lean and forward momentum so that to keep from falling on your face the rear leg must be brought forward to support your body weight.

Remember to keep the front toe in contact with the ground throughout the toss and serving. This will insure that you do not foot fault and also will provide a firm support base for hitting.

THE TOSS

Unless you are a two handed hitter, two balls should always be carried in the nonracket hand on the first serve of every point. The

Stance

ball being hit should be pushed into the air (not thrown) to a height equal or slightly greater than can be reached with the racket arm fully extended. It can not be stressed too highly that serving faults are almost always caused by an **inaccurate ball toss,** thus it becomes most important that you learn to toss the ball exactly where you wish it to go at all times. The toss should be made so that the ball is thrown to a height at least the distance of a fully extended racket arm, and if allowed to drop, it should land about one foot to the right of your front toe and about one foot inside the court. This toss, which is slightly to the right of your body, will insure that sufficient slicing of the ball can occur. If the toss is not to the right it will be nearly impossible to impart the necessary side spin slicing action necessary to the serve.

The serve itself is generally broken down into three phases — the toss and backswing, the forward swing, and the follow-through.

1. **The backswing.** The tossing arm and racket arm should begin the serve at least waist high with the ball hand touching the racket head. (See figure.) As the left arm goes up, the racket arm drops down in a scissors or rocker motion, with the edge of the racket face leading. As the ball is released the racket head begins an arc which brings it to a position behind the server's back with the elbow and wrist not yet cocked or bent. At this point the elbow and wrist begin to cock allowing the racket head to move to a downward position almost touching the middle of the server's back.

2. **The forward swing.** As the ball descends the body weight shifts to the front foot, while the trunk and shoulders begin a forward rotation. As the wrist and elbow snap forward the racket arm is fully extended at point of impact. The motion is often compared to throwing a ball or throwing one's racket into the proper service area.

Toss

Impact point

Follow-through

3. **The follow-through.** The follow-through is simply a continuation of the forward swing making sure that the racket head ends up on the opposite side of your body and that the wrist fully uncocks so that it is pointing in the direction of the fence behind you and slightly downward. The right or back foot will cross the baseline to assist in maintaining body balance.

MOST COMMON MISTAKES OF SLICE SERVE

1. *The ball is not thrown as high as can be reached with the extended racket arm.*
2. *The ball is not hit at the full extension point, but is allowed to drop a foot or more before hitting.*
3. *The ball is not thrown far enough to the right to allow the necessary slicing action.*
4. *The wrist and elbow are not fully cocked. The check point is "scratching the back."*

THE SLICE SERVE

THE FLAT SERVE

Most professionals rely upon the Eastern grip to hit the flat or no spin serve. As the name implies, the ball is hit with the racket face square to the ball as opposed to attempting to cut off the right hand corner as in the slice serve. The old axiom, "less spin more speed" certainly holds true here. The two serves might also be compared with throwing an overhand fast ball and a semi-sidearm curve. The key factor in causing the racket face to meet the ball squarely is the angle that you cock your wrist. If the wrist is bent straight back and brought straight through then the ball will be hit with little or no spin. On the other hand, if you cock the wrist at an angle and snap through with a twist, as a curve ball pitcher does, then you will impart a slicing or spinning motion to the ball.

Whereas the flat serve is very effective for reasonably tall — six feet or over — players, most short players will probably have more success with the slice serve. Remember also that to hit the flat serve the ball must be tossed more off the left toe and not as far to the right as in the slice serve.

THE FLAT SERVE

THE AMERICAN TWIST SERVE

The American Twist or topspin serve is probably the toughest serve to master since it requires an unnatural arm motion. Its value lies in its use as a second serve which has a high kicking action into the opponents backhand, and for doubles play, since the high bounce allows the server more time to come in behind the serve.

To execute the serve, place the racket in an Eastern *backhand* grip. The ball must be tossed slightly behind the body and in back of the head. As the racket face moves to make contact, the server must hit up on the ball and at the same time snap the wrist hard over the top of the ball. Since the ball is tossed slightly behind the body, this will cause the server to bend backwards more, but will also cause an upward hitting motion. The impact point on the tennis ball should be at 10 or 11 o'clock and with a topward rolling wrist motion. This motion resembles a brushing upward movement on the back of one's head. The follow-through is to the right side of the body.

THE AMERICAN TWIST SERVE

PRACTICE HINTS FOR SERVING

1. Move in about halfway to the net and practice throwing a tennis ball into the proper service area. Throw vigorously using considerable wrist snap.
2. Now throw for the corners of the service area.
3. Gradually move back until you are on the baseline.
4. Practice the serving motion in front of a mirror. If the ceilings are too low use a table tennis paddle as a substitute for your racket.
5. Take a basket of balls and back off from the fence approximately 38 feet. Mark the fence either with an imaginary three-foot high line or attach several pieces of white tape in a line. Serve over the tape.
6. If you are having trouble serving from the baseline, move in about halfway — to the back service line. As speed and accuracy improve gradually back away until you are again behind the baseline.
7. Place racket covers or empty ball cans in critical serving areas and attempt to hit them with your serve.
8. The most important thing is to carry a basket or sack of old balls with you each time you go to the courts. Before leaving, always hit at least one sack full.
9. If you are having trouble synchronizing your toss and backswing, try tossing with the racket already cocked behind your back. Remember to take it all the way back to the "backscratching" position. Also, remember that this procedure is only a temporary measure and that eventually it will be to your advantage to take a full windup.

A COMPARISON CHART FOR SERVING

	FLAT	SLICE	AMERICAN TWIST
Grip	Eastern	Continental	Eastern Backhand
Ball Toss	Off front toe ½ to 1 foot in court	To right of front toe ½ to 1 foot in court	To left of and behind head
Position of Wrist	Straight back "fly swatter position"	At an angle as a curve ball pitcher	An upward rolling motion
Ball Impact Point	12-1 o'clock	1-2 o'clock	12-1 o'clock
Effect on Ball	Little or no spin great speed	Less speed than flat. Ball kicks to left. Great spin and low bounce	Decreased speed. Very high topspin bounce

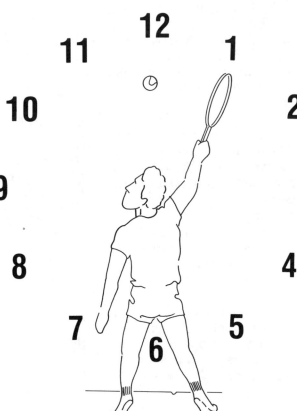

SERVICE CHECK LIST

NAME:_____ *P* =Poor   *F* =Fair   *G* =Good ( )

Divide Service courts in half — 10 serves to each area.
Check the appropriate box as you observe your partner demonstrate his/
her ability to serve. Watch several serves to determine accuracy in record-
ing your observations.

1. Footwork alignment is proper at the baseline.	P F G
2. Proper grip is used for serve being attempted.	P F G
3. Release of ball on toss is at correct arm extension.	P F G
4. Height of toss is about 1 foot above racket reach.	P F G
5. Toss uses no wrist or *elbow* motion as lift is made.	P F G
6. Weight shifts properly into the stroke.	P F G
7. Elbow bends fully on racket backswing.	P F G
8. Ball is hit at full extension of arm.	P F G
9. Slight wrist action used at contact.	P F G
10. Follow-through is across the body.	P F G
11. Is the service placement satisfactory?	P F G
12. Is there spin on the ball?	P F G
13. Is there sufficient speed to keep the receiver deep?	P F G

COMMENTS:_____

_____

_____

_____

CHAPTER 9 EVALUATION

1. Which service is considered the basic service for reliability and consistency?

2. Name the three types of service, and explain how each differs with reference to stance, grip, ball toss, backswing, contact and follow-through.

3. Which serve is frequently used in doubles?

4. As a second serve, this service is most popular.

5. How would you describe the "backscratch" position used by better players?

6. Describe the body at the instant of contact in the flat service.

7. What is the No. 1 fault of most servers, when common mistakes are made?

8. Where is the follow-through for the topspin (twist) service?

9. Using the clock dial as a reference, complete the following:

   a. 12:00_____(type of service)

   b. 1:00_____

   c. 1:30_____

10. Explain the tossing arm — when is the ball released, what motion is used, where should the trajectory of the ball go?

CHAPTER 10

AUXILIARY STROKES

In addition to the three basic strokes — forehand, backhand and service, there are several other types of returns that must be made by the player. Primarily, these are the Volley, the Smash or Overhead, the Lob, and the Half Volley. As a player becomes proficient in the basic three, the opportunity presents itself to enlarge the depth of the strategy in his game. This is done through adequate use of patterns of attack and defense, developed through the execution of these auxiliary strokes. A good player cannot be without them.

THE VOLLEY

The volley is the stroke used to return a ball before it comes into contact with the court. It is usually made from an opponent's drive. It is a relatively simple shot that becomes more complicated as the tempo of the game increases.

Usually a volley is made in the forecourt area — that is, closer to the net, and well within the service court. It is an offensive stroke, often winning the point outright. Due to the close position to the net, an angle can be obtained in the volley that frequently prohibits a return by the opponent. Thus, its effectiveness as an offensive weapon.

THE GRIP

Beginners and intermediates will find greater comfort in using the Eastern forehand and backhand grips when hitting a volley. This grip has already been learned, is comfortable, and adapts itself readily to the stroke. Eliminate all wrist action.

For high intermediates and advanced players, a service grip — halfway between the Eastern forehand and backhand grip — is pre-

BASIC VOLLEY POSITIONS I

ferred. This is primarily due to the increased tempo of the game which prohibits a grip change while at the net. Experimentation and practice will determine which is best for the player according to the style and agressiveness of that particular individual.

FOOTWORK

The footwork patterns for the forehand and the backhand volleys are identical — just on opposite sides of the body. In most situations the player will use a basic forward pivot explained earlier. A slight bending of the knees will prove to be helpful as the execution is made.

Since the player is at the net position, there are times when the pace of the balls' approach will not allow proper footwork because of lack of time. In situations like this — and there are many of them — footwork is restricted and concentration on racket position is more important. A "check stop" motion of the player will aid greatly in controlling the volley. This is simply coming to a brief pause just prior to making the intended shot. By pausing, you are able to concentrate on your volley. The "check stop" is used on the approach to the net.

The volley position can be a vulnerable one if the approach shots and volleys are not well executed. Also, the opponent will attempt passing shots to either side that will cause additional court coverage for the net player. In situations like this, coverage is made as illustrated below.

BASIC VOLLEY POSITIONS II

Cross-over step. A step and a pivot of the right foot and a large step across with the left foot, parallel to the net. This is accompanied by a rapid extension of the racket into the path of the ball.

This pattern will allow almost all of the court to be covered using a comfortable, basic style of footwork. When used on the backhand side simply reverse the procedure.

STROKE TECHNIQUE

The volley is not a stroke in the context of a forehand or a backhand. It is a stroke that utilizes a blocking motion into the incoming ball. As the ball approaches, hold the racket by the correct grip and move the face of the racket into the path of the ball. A short backswing, about a foot in length, is permitted. Contact the ball with a short "punch." Aim the ball downward into the opponent's court, deep, and at a sharp angle. A tight grip is mandatory to stabilize the stroke and to cope with the impact of the incoming ball.

When receiving balls that are above the net, an attempt should be made to punch through the ball at a downward angle. Care must be used to clear the net sufficiently. On volleys made from below the height of the net, the player must exercise caution as the return flight of the ball must be angled upward. This may cause the ball to go out-of-bounds if the hitter is careless. As the ball approaches, the

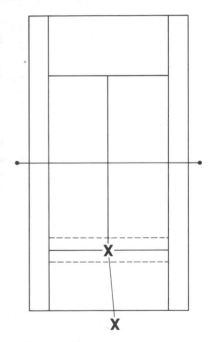

Court positions for volley approach

hitter bends the knees to "get down" with the ball. An effort should be made to keep the racket head and hand at the same level, parallel to the ground, on both the low backhand and forehand volley. As contact is made, a very firm grip is maintained, causing the blocking effect on the ball. There is very little follow-through used.

COURT POSITION

Singles. As the player receives the opportunity to go to the net, he returns the short ball away from the opponent. This is usually to an open part of the court and at an angle away from the other player. The direction of the approach shot will determine the position of the net player. The approach shot should have good pace and be deep to the open area of the court. If the receiver is in the home position, place the approach shot deep to the backhand corner, as this is frequently the weakest side, and many players are unable to handle the pressure created by the approaching net rusher.

When receiving a short ball as you go to the net you must use caution in executing the approach shot. This is due to the following reasons: (1) frequently the ball will be below the height of the net; (2) the distance between the point of contact and the opponent's baseline has now become shortened, due to your advancement to the net. Thus, when the total body weight is moved forward in a running pattern it is extremely easy to overhit the ball causing the shot to go out of bounds.

As the approach shot is made, the hitter positions about eight feet from the net, on the side in which the ball is hit but close to the midcourt line. This position will allow maximum court coverage for a player. For approach shots that may go down the middle, the only position to obtain is one in the center of the forecourt area.

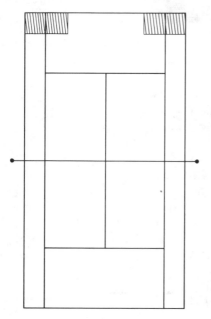

Approach shot zones

Doubles. The volley position in doubles is slightly different than that for singles since there are two players covering the court. Each player, being responsible for their side, should position themselves halfway between the doubles side-line and the midcourt line. Ideally, both players assume the net position together — the server/receiver joining his partner at the net. Coverage of all shots should be complete if both players work harmoniously together. Remember that all shots going down the center should be taken by the player with the forehand return. Each player should practice conscientiously so that the point can be won quickly, rather than to simply keep the ball in play. Make your shot crisp and sharp. In doubles, aim at an angle that will win the point outright, particularly down the center, between opponents. If this is not practiced, then aim your volley at the feet of the closest net player.

COMMON VOLLEY ERRORS

Volley goes too long (out of bounds). Tighten your grip and restrict the amount of backswing used to punch the ball. Also, limit the amount of follow-through, as this stroking effect will tend to increase the length of your ball.

Volley has no speed or crispness. Prepare earlier so you can meet the ball in front of the body — both backhand and forehand. Anticipate well, step into the shot. Watch the ball closely, contacting the ball in the center of the racket face.

Defensive body volleys lacking pace. Use your backhand volley and grip. Move your feet into better position and try to step into the ball as it approaches. Contact the ball well out in front. Anticipate early.

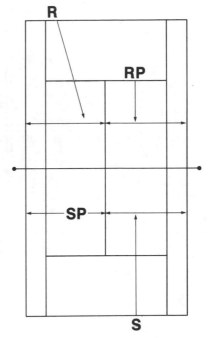

Court positions for volley in doubles

TIPS ON TECHNIQUE

1. Move into position quickly. Try to stabilize your footwork before your opponent hits the ball.
2. Select your grip preference early, and learn its strengths and weaknesses.
3. If possible, step into your shot.
4. Be sure to contact the ball out in front of the body — forehand and backhand.
5. Use a very firm grip — no wrist action, please!
6. Restrict the backswing and the follow-through. *"Punch the ball."*
7. Bend the knees for low balls, keeping your hand and the racket head parallel to the court if possible.
8. Aim for depth and a good angle.

THE OVERHEAD SMASH

When you are playing the net in the forecourt position and your opponent hits a short high ball, easily within reach, you should react by preparing to hit the smash, or overhead, as it is commonly called. This is the most spectacular shot of tennis. The overhead is used frequently to win the point outright. Although the shot can be hit from any position on the court, the chances for error become much greater as the player approaches the backcourt area. The closer to the net the better, as the angles are greater, and the height of the bounce can be effective, sometimes going over the reach of the racket of the opponent.

THE GRIP

The basic grip for the overhead is the Eastern forehand grip. This is primarily due to the familiarity already established with the forehand. Other grips may be used, including the service grip, obtaining a grip halfway between the forehand and the backhand and the Eastern backhand grip. The latter is used primarily by advanced players. The timing is

THE SHORT OVERHEAD

more critical, however, and the grip causes a closed face on the racket, pulling the ball sharply down into the opponent's court. The grip style will depend largely on the playing skill of the user. As more skill is obtained, the player will move to either the slice grip or the backhand.

FOOTWORK

As in any stroke in tennis, footwork becomes one of the most important ingredients. Proper execution of footwork will move the player into position to play the ball correctly.

In preparing to use the overhead, the footwork begins as soon as the high arc of the incoming ball is recognized. Preparation begins with analyzing where the ball will be hit, and moving your body to this particular area.

The initial movement should be to turn sideways to the net and to the incoming ball. Using the basic side-step motion, move back under the ball, keeping the ball in front of the body at all times. At a point where you anticipate the ball will land, place the weight on both feet, favoring the rear foot primarily. As the stroke is made, shift the weight forward into the stroke, straightening the knees as the reach is extended into the ball. Concentrate on keeping the feet at a 45 degree angle to the

THE SCISSOR KICK OVERHEAD

net and to the ball, as you shift the body forward. This position will be a comfortable one as it closely resembles the serving position.

STROKE TECHNIQUE

Basic preparation for most tennis strokes consists of the backswing, the contact point, and the follow-through. This is also true for the overhead.

Since the original position is at the net, it is assumed that a ready position is maintained. First change the grip. The initial movement is to turn sideways to the net, taking the racket back into the drop-back position behind the back. With the other arm, point toward the incoming ball. This motion is excellent for balance. Continue the racket in the backswing position, elbow high, racket head dipping well below the back. As the ball approaches the contact point, swing the racket head upward toward the ball. Contact the ball slightly out in front of the body at about "one o'clock." Bring the wrist into the ball very slightly to get the angle down onto the court. An effort should be made to hit **up** and over the ball, rather than "down" on to the ball. The follow-through will be to the opposite side of the body. Recovery should be quick, as many overheads are returned.

OVERHEAD COURT POSITION

Usually the court position is in the forecourt area. Most overheads are hit from the service courts. Of course, the stroke may be hit from any part of the court, and this is frequently done. However, for best success, the player will achieve more consistency, accuracy and placement by staying relatively close to the net. For very high incoming balls, the wise player will allow the ball to bounce before hitting the overhead. This will provide for better timing in the execution.

Use of the overhead in both singles and doubles will depend entirely on the effectiveness of the offensive and defensive strokes. Strategy will also play a very important part in maneuvering the opponent into positions where the lob will be used, as it is this stroke that causes the overhead to come into play.

TIPS ON TECHNIQUE

1. Keep your eye on the ball at all times and "point the ball in" with the opposite hand.
2. Take the racket back early, behind the back.
3. Don't "get set" too early, keep moving the feet.
4. Stroke smoothly and aggressively.
5. Lead with the racket head, use your wrist.
6. Contact the ball with the arm at a full extension.
7. Follow through with the racket to the left side (diagonally across).
8. Recover quickly in case of a return by your opponent.
9. Practice frequently, using more power as control is established.

COMMON ERRORS

Ball usually goes long. The ball is hit early and the racket is making contact before the ball passes "one o'clock." The racket face is "open" at contact. Concentrate on hitting with enough wrist to bring the ball down.

Ball goes into the net frequently. Stroke upward into the ball more strongly. Be sure to drop the racket head behind the back before the upward swing.

No power into the ball. Bend the elbow totally, and throw the racket upward into the ball. Utilize the wrist more effectively.

THE LOB

If you can picture in your mind the arc of a rainbow, you can visualize the trajectory of the lob. This is probably one of the least used and practiced strokes in tennis. It is not a complicated shot but most players would rather use another stroke when trying to get away from a difficult problem — such as being pressed deep to a corner.

The lob can be either offensive or defensive. However, it is used primarily as a defensive shot. It is rarely practiced to the degree that the technique is mastered. The well executed lob can be most discomforting to an opponent. The main objectives in lobbing are:

1. to give yourself more time to recover
2. push the opponent(s) away from the net
3. change of pace in your game plan

THE GRIP

Use either the Eastern forehand or backhand grip, as previously discussed. The lob is actually either a forehand or a backhand ground stroke so the grip will follow the respective shot.

FOOTWORK

As with any ground stroke, proper footwork will greatly aid in determining successful execution. Earlier discussions on proper patterns of footwork should be followed. We should mention that when the player is "set" in the correct position, there is a much stronger chance that the shot will be hit firmly, achieve the proper height, and obtain sufficient depth to be effective.

STROKING TECHNIQUE

As stated earlier, getting into position is of utmost importance. When the incoming ball approaches, move into position as early as possible. Try to have the racket back by the time the ball bounces. From the backswing position, with knees bent, bring the racket slightly under the ball as your forward swing begins. By hitting upward on the shot, lift and height will be achieved.

When you are approaching the contact point with the ball, begin to lift rapidly as though your follow-through is starting now. This will create a high arch on the shot, sufficient to clear the forecourt position occupied by the opponent. By dropping the racket head earlier, more height can be reached, if this is desirable.

The follow-through is most important, as it will serve to guide the ball in the intended direction and height. The follow-through is also used to put spin on the ball.

It should be noted that the normal stroking technique remains the same as a regular forehand or backhand. Comfort in the grip, wrist and elbow is most desirable. The lob is an arm stroke, using the entire arm and racket as one moving extension to **STROKE** the ball. Restrict the use of the wrist as much as possible.

OFFENSIVE VS DEFENSIVE

Both types of lobs are very effective when used properly. The primary differences are found in the direction, disguise, height and spin of the ball. The offensive lob is used as a weapon against an unsuspecting opponent. The stroke can be an outright point winner.

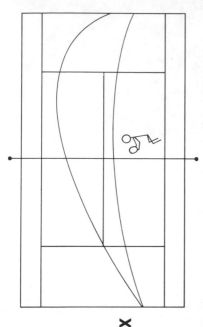

Offensive and defensive lobs

Target area for all lobs

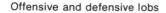

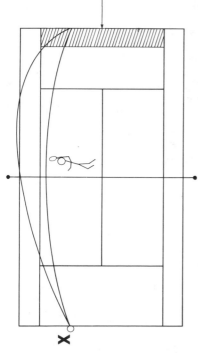

The defensive lob, on the other hand is usually anticipated by the opponent due to the situation at hand. That is to say, you are being pressed, and need more time to recover. So you send a defensive lob up into the air, deep to the backcourt.

By definition, an *offensive lob* is one in which the lob is well disguised with a normal forehand or backhand back swing. However, as the racket meets the ball, a lift is provided that creates moderate topspin. The trajectory causes the ball to go over the outstretched racket reach of the opponent.

When the ball hits the ground, the topspin causes the ball to "jump" away from the net, making a most difficult shot to return. Used discreetly, it is very effective if executed well. If the shot is not hit well, it will probably fall short, well within the reach of the opponent.

On the other side of the picture, the defensive lob is a much less disguised stroke. The attacking player knows that the defensive lob is a frequently used shot to nullify an effective net approach. While the defensive lob is easier to return than the offensive lob, the return can usually be handled comfortably due to the height of the lob. You should recognize that the defensive lob should land deep in the backcourt area, close to the baseline.

When attempting either lob, it is best to aim your shot toward the *backhand corner* of the opponent. This is the weakest area of return and if your stroke is short, your opponent will have trouble putting the ball away on the high backhand shot. Many times, when the opponent can reach the ball, he carefully drives it over using an uncomfortable high volley. This can easily be a set up for the alert lobber. Be prepared for this possibility. However, if the lob is to the forehand, a return is somewhat easier to achieve and, if the shot is low and within reach — watch out for the overhead that is sure to come. Remember, practice makes a big difference.

TIPS ON TECHNIQUE

1. Get into position quickly.
2. Use proper footwork.
3. Disguise your intentions if possible.
4. Stroke firmly upward into the ball, using a full follow-through.
5. Keep the racket "on the ball" as long as possible.
6. Recover quickly for the return.

COMMON ERRORS

Lobs are too short. Secure your position earlier. Use the arm more in making the stroke. Drive up and through the ball. Follow through fully. "Carry" the ball on the strings as long as possible.

Ball is mis-hit often. Get ready earlier. Watch the ball more closely. See the ball into the strings of the racket.

Offensive lobs are frequently "put away." Don't "go to the well" too often. Be discreet and use it sparingly, preferably from inside the baseline. The deeper you are when you use it, the more time the opponent has to reach the ball due to the low trajectory.

HALF-VOLLEY

The half-volley is primarily a defensive shot that is neither a volley nor a full ground stroke. It is utilized when you are caught in a court position with the ball bouncing at your feet.

THE HALF-VOLLEY

This predicament occurs most often on the advance to a net position and when you become caught in "no man's land." Another word for the half-volley might be the "trap shot" since a player simply places the racket behind the anticipated point of bounce and allows the ball to deflect from the racket face. The stroke is adjusted by keeping both backswing and follow-through to a minimum. Most of the power for the shot is provided by the ball's rebound speed. The point of impact should be slightly in front of your body.

Another analogy that might be used for this shot is the play of a baseball infielder. Often times infielders will have to "stab with their gloves" at a point where they think the ball will rebound from the playing field. The difference between baseball and tennis being that you have a racket rather than a glove.

The grip for this half-volley should be the same as for the forehand and backhand. Remember to use a "check stop" approach as is required in the volley, keeping the knees bent and the head of the racket nearly parallel to the ground. Also, a short backswing followed by a short follow-through is necessary as you continue to the net position.

The angle at which you hold the racket face will determine the ball's angle of deflection. Of course the closer you are to the net the more you will have to open the face of the racket to raise the ball. A backcourt half-volley will require the face of the racket to be more closed to prevent the ball from rising too high. Remember to have patience since most beginning tennis players will find that mastery of this shot requires considerable practice.

CHAPTER 10 EVALUATION

1. Contrast the volley stroke opposed to a regular forehand or backhand stroke.

2. Discuss the pros and cons of the Continental grip.

3. What is a "check stop" and how should it be used in volleying?

4. List two common weaknesses of the volley shot and techniques to employ for their correction.

5. What is the value of the overhead smash?

6. What would you suggest to the person who generally hits long on the overhead?

7. What about the overhead that constantly goes in the net?

8. Contrast the offensive and defensive lob shot.

9. Define "half-volley" and describe.

CHAPTER 11

SINGLES STRATEGY

THE PERCENTAGE THEORY

"If I can somehow manage to hit one more ball back than you, I'll win this point." This is the philosophy of the tennis player who attempts to pursue the percentage theory. The importance of keeping the ball in play should be paramount in the mind of every player. It is understandable that this is sometimes very hard to do, and cannot be accomplished at all times.

It is a well known fact that most tennis matches are won on errors. This means that the average and sometimes above average players tend to defeat themselves by simply making too many mistakes. These players seem content to hit one or two balls back, then impatience gets the best of them and they try to force an opening, but don't have the tools with which to do it. Thus, they make an error, and this gives the opponent another point.

In good tennis circles, the player who makes the fewest errors or mistakes will usually win. In a match between players A and B, a close analysis would show that if A is the winner, close to 80% of the points won by A are due to common errors by B. This should tell us something. The 20% or so of the points won by A on forcing shots, placements, or aces, are not sufficient to cause much of a problem. Realizing this, we know we must reduce our careless mistakes.

Careless mistakes occur in the entire range of skills that go into the game — from watching the ball, footwork, to stroke technique, and strategy. To be a "pusher," as we call the retriever, is a true compliment.

Most players who find themselves on the opposing side of the net from the pusher know they are in for a long day. They will either have to settle back and play the same game as the pusher — a task they have neither the skill nor patience to achieve, or they must attack and defeat the pusher using placement, power, and a forcing type game. Not many players have expertise for these tools either. So after several hours of play the pusher will usually emerge smiling while the opponent stomps off or slinks away talking to himself.

To play percentage tennis, a person must develop an optimum level of conditioning, for this requires a tremendous amount of running to keep the ball in play. A full knowledge of techniques will be necessary, as correct execution will be demanded in the strokes. A sound knowledge of strategy is also expected since the retriever will find it useful to understand the intent of the opposing player and be able to counter this with correct strokes that work to his purpose.

Remember that this is not an easy undertaking. It requires all of the qualities mentioned above, plus great determination. The primary ingredients of percentage tennis are patience and conditioning. Without patience the percentage theory is not a realistic goal.

THE DEPTH THEORY

Simply stated, this involves the consistent practice of stroking the ball deep into the opponent's backcourt. It is very effective to keep your opponent from mounting an attack against you. Imagine being in your home position, two feet behind the baseline. Your opponent strokes a deep ball that lands just inside the line. You have two choices: (1) to back up, giving ground, and play the return from six to eight feet deep or (2) to play the ball, using a half-volley stroke, from your present position. Your choice will be mandated by your skill level and perhaps the pace of the incoming ball.

An aggressive player wants to begin attacking the opponent at the earliest opportunity, knowing that this additional pressure *by itself* frequently creates a stroking error. The strategy of the attacker is to wait for a short ball, move in on it, hit an effective approach shot, and secure the net position. By keeping the ball deep, you will accomplish several things:

1. You will keep the opponent away from the net (attack) position.
2. You will allow yourself more time to prepare for each stroke, since the incoming ball is hit from the opponent's backcourt.
3. You will provide yourself added opportunities to go "on the attack," since your opponent's depth in the backcourt will cause him to hit many short returns.
4. Your court position will become more secure, since the possible angles of return will become smaller due to the depth of the hitter.
5. If you hustle, you will realize that from this depth the opponent cannot score an ace on placement against you, simply because he (she) cannot establish the critical angle or speed desired. The shot is hit from too far away and it must travel too far in the air before it reaches your side of the net. The length of the shot provides you with the time needed to make another successful return.

The depth theory is especially pertinent in volleying. You will want to hit the ball away from the opponent, and deep to the backcourt area, allowing little or no time for a return shot. Short angles are excellent, provided they win the point outright. However, short angles, and careless volleys that land in the middle of the court, create havoc for any net player, and frequently cause the loss of the point. It is an uncomfortable feeling, after establishing a position at the net, to volley short and bring the opponent to the attack zone. You begin to feel like a target, and are rightly intimidated. Remember, keep the volley deep and stay out of trouble.

COURT POSITION

Since the basic "home position" is one to three feet behind the center mark, most players will return to this area after hitting the ball. As you become more proficient in your game, part of this success will be due to increased anticipation through observation of the opponent. That is, you will suspect that your opponent will stroke the ball to the open court area rather than directly back to you. This is the same strategy you are also using. Careful observation of the footwork and body position of your opponent will tell you the direction in which the stroke is intended. However, since you cannot be 100% positive of this, you must anticipate all possibilities.

Bisecting the angles of return. When you do this, you are splitting the distance between where the ball can be hit — to your right and left, with you in the center of that angle. This is true on service as well as ground strokes and volleys. Thus, when properly positioned, you will have equal distance to cover on forehand and backhand.

Observe where your opponent stands when receiving service and during play. Frequently he will be standing much to the left of the center of the angle discussed above. This will probably indicate a weak backhand and an attempt to cover for it.

No-man's land. Generally, tennis play occurs in either the backcourt area, or at the net. Beginners and intermediates will stay in the backcourt while advanced players will develop the serve and volley game. The normal drive coming over the net will land within a yard of the service line, in the area commonly referred to as "no man's land." This area is between the baseline (backcourt) area and the volley (forecourt) position. Young or inexperienced players frequently play in this area, making it their home position. The problem

No-man's land

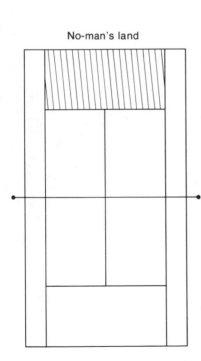

lies with the situation where incoming balls may either land right at your feet or may go by you as much as head high. This creates anxiety in returning the low shots successfully and in determining if those going past you — still in the air — are going to go out of bounds or are they going to land inside the court. Luck seems to say that those high ones you hit would have gone out, and those you let go always drop inside the baseline. If you play in "no man's land," pointwise, "you get killed"! Also, since your position is not close enough to the net to effectively volley the ball and you are not deep enough to allow sufficient time to properly position yourself, you can easily be the recipient of sharp crosscourt strokes, or drives that go down the line.

Frequently you must come into the "no man's land" area to play a short ball. Once you play it, however, you must continue on into the net, or return to your baseline. **Do not remain in the center of the court.**

No-man's land

Right service court

SERVING POSITIONS

Left service court

SERVICE STRATEGY

PICKING THE RIGHT SERVE

As we have observed earlier, there are three basic serves. They are the flat serve, the slice serve and the twist or topspin. Every advanced player should develop the ability to properly execute each serve. Often one type of service is more effective than another against an opponent. The player will benefit greatly if he/she can discover which type gives the opponent the most trouble, and can then use this serve to maximum benefit.

On the right side of the baseline, the server will usually stand from one to three feet from the center mark. This position will be maintained no matter which serve is used. This angle will promote service to the opponent's backhand and will allow for proper court coverage on service returns. It is permissable to stand as far to the right as the singles sideline, although this is rarely done due to the amount of court area left open on the backhand side.

When serving from the left side of the baseline, the server's position is about three to five feet from the center mark. Most players will stand a little farther away from the center mark on this side due to: (1) a desire to get a sharper angle toward the opponent's backhand and (2) a feeling of more security toward the forehand side for returned serves.

Generally the keynote to serving is *variety*. You will find a significant advantage in hitting different types of serves to your opponent. You should determine very early in a match which serve seems to give your opponent the most difficulty, and use this serve most of the time. Hit about 85% of your serves to the **backhand** of the receiver, as this in itself will usually create many errors in service returns. Also, many returns from poor backhands will be so weak that they can easily be attacked.

Vary the type of service used. If your favorite serve is a slice service to the backhand, occasionally use a topspin, or flat serve just to change the pace. This will often throw the opponent off insofar as timing and positioning are concerned, thus creating an error. Move your opponent around as you serve. Place most serves to the backhand, some to the forehand, and some directly into the body. The slice service toward the backhand that curves into the body is extremely effective when used discreetly.

Frequently the first and second serve vary greatly. Many inexperienced players serve very hard, inaccurate balls on the first effort, then follow by a very slow paced ball that, while secure from a double fault, does not do anything other than to put the point in play. This type of serve can easily be handled by the receiver, who usually puts the server on the defensive by hitting a solid, well placed return.

Logic will show that a better procedure to follow will be to have two serves of about the same speed, but with different types of spin; for example, a flat first serve, followed by a slice or a topspin serve. Another combination is to use a slice service as a first serve, followed by a twist (topspin) serve. The use of spin — either slice or topspin — gives more clearance to the ball as it goes over the net. As a result, it is more secure against the double fault.

Remember these basic points: (1) *Placement* — getting the ball deep to the opponent's backhand, right at the opponent or to the forehand corner (2) *Speed* — sufficient speed to keep the opponent in the backcourt area when returning your serve and (3) *Spin* — enough to allow the ball to clear the net, then to take the ball down on the court, and enough spin to curve the ball in the desired direction (slice) or to kick up a higher bounce on contact with the court (twist).

There are times when variety or change is necessary. Although you have a good serve, if you constantly serve to the same spot again and again, your opponent will adjust, and begin returning more effectively against you. So keep your opponent guessing.

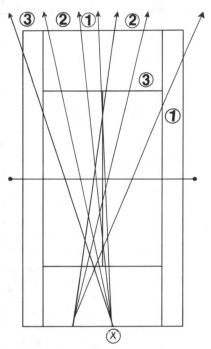

Placement of service

Forehand and backhand courts

If you use serve and volley tactics as your basic strategy, you must debate whether a speed or a spin serve is most effective against your opponent. If the opponent handles your speed well, he may return the ball before you can establish your position for the approach volley. Thus, a slower spin serve might be more advantageous. On the other hand, if your favorite serve is a spin serve, but due to the slower speed your opponent handles it easily and causes you to make errors due to his return, you have the other problem. There are things you must "feel" out as you begin playing the match. Think the problem through. Then do whatever is best in the given situation.

If you are primarily a baseline player — you stay in the backcourt area — you are part of the large majority of tennis players. The baseline player uses the service as a means of starting the point. Granted, the serve is hit as hard as control will allow (sometimes harder!) On occasion this will win the point by itself. However, most of the time the player will use his/her ground strokes to win the point, coming to the net only as a matter of necessity when a very short ball is received. Beginning and intermediate tennis is played with this strategy in mind.

STRATEGY WHEN RECEIVING SERVICE

As your opponent prepares to serve to you, you will probably have many things going through your mind.

"Where should I stand?" "What type of serve will he use?" "Will the server come to the net?" "How fast will the serve be hit?"

If you worry slightly about these things, welcome to the vast majority of serious tennis players.

Many leading tennis professionals agree that the service is the most important stroke in tennis. If this is true, and we have no reason to doubt it, then the service return must be equally as important from the receiver's point of view. We know that in good tennis if you can win the games you serve and break the opponent's serve one time, you will win the set. Thus, being able to return serve effectively is extremely important. Here are the key points in returning service:

1. *Place the ball in play.* Try not to make an error on the return. This is the most important factor in receiving service. Give the opponent a chance to make an error. **RETURN THE BALL.**

2. Maintain a court position according to the opponent's serve. Remember to bisect the angle of return, allowing equal coverage to the forehand and the backhand. (See figure.)

3. If the opponent stays at the baseline, try for a medium speed return that is to the backcourt area. If you can do this effectively, the service advantage is lost. Now you can concentrate on playing out the point. If you get a short return, drive deep to the backhand corner and then take the net position.

4. If the opponent uses a serve and volley strategy follow these points:

   a. *Stay calm,* concentrate, anticipate the serve.

   b. *Keep the return low* — usually to the feet of the server at the service line as he comes toward the net. Move in on the service if you can to cut down on the time the server has to get to the net.

   c. If the service is hard, with spin, just try to *block it* back with a slight chip using backspin. Disregard using a full groundstroke technique. Try for a low return.

   d. Aim the ball down the sideline. This will cause the server to change directions on the approach. However, if you go to the center of the court due to lack of time for preparation of your return, this is satisfactory.

   e. Be ready to attack the opponent's approach shot. If you hit a good service return, you can capitalize on

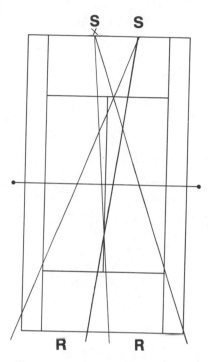

Bisecting angles of return (service)

your next shot. Use lobs and drives effectively now.

f. Occasionally use the lob to throw the opponent off guard. Lob toward the backhand side.

g. Be consistent, don't make careless errors. Give your opponent the opportunity to beat himself. Patience is required.

TYPES OF GAMES

A tennis player's skill will determine the styles of play that may be used effectively. These are determined primarily by the competency established in practice patterns using the strokes of the game.

1. 3-Stroke Game — uses the service, forehand and backhand only. This is played as a baseline game, whether singles or doubles.

2. 5-Stroke Game — uses the three strokes mentioned above, plus the volley and the smash. This is a more aggressive style of play frequently found in intermediate tennis.

3. All Court Game — uses all of the strokes mentioned above, plus the auxiliary shots including the offensive and defensive lobs, half-volley, chop and drop shots, lob volley and the drop volley. There are not many intermediate players who have a good command of all of these strokes, and probably very few advanced players. This skill level is primarily found in higher levels of competitive play. Even then, many of these shots are not used effectively.

Remember, no matter what your style of play, there is always plenty of room for improvement.

CHAPTER 11 EVALUATION

1. Most tennis matches are lost, rather than won. Explain.

2. When two players meet on the court, the winner will usually have a large percentage of points "given" to him by the loser. What percentage of points would this total?

3. List several items a player should concentrate on to correct a poor percentage of returns.

4. What should the philosophy be of the player who expounds on the percentage theory in tennis?

5. Explain the depth theory. How can it assist you in becoming a better player? List several strategy points associated with the depth theory.

6. What is meant by bisecting the angle of return?

7. How can you utilize the service as an effective weapon against your opponent? List several strategy points that will easily mean points for you if you follow them.

8. If the server does not come to the net following the service, what should you attempt on the return. If the server comes in, what should you do?

9. As receiver of the service, your first thought should be to do what?

10. Define the following:
    a. 3-stroke game
    b. 5-stroke game
    c. All court game

CHAPTER 12

THE DOUBLES GAME

DOUBLES STRATEGY

The game of doubles is a team sport. Granted, there are only two members on the team, but when play begins you are very much supportive of each other, as players would be in any sport. There are several ways that singles and doubles differ.

a. The court is nine feet wider in doubles, bringing the alleys into use.

b. Both players share equal responsibility in covering the court space.

c. General strategy involves both players going into the "attack" (net) position as quickly as possible, and playing side by side.

d. Dependence upon your partner to adequately keep **you** out of trouble with his strokes.

e. Groundstrokes become less important in doubles. The serve, volley, and overhead are the strokes most often used.

f. Placement of shots is more critical in doubles since an effort must be made to keep the ball away from the player(s) at the net.

g. Doubles is a much faster game, with drives being cut off by net volleys, and sharp angles being hit.

A broader variety of strokes is utilized in doubles. This requires that doubles players practice all shots frequently so that when called upon to use them, they will be readily available.

There are three types of doubles games played today. They are basic doubles, Australian doubles and "club" or recreational doubles. These three vary in technique, court positions, and strategy.

BASIC DOUBLES

Court positions for basic doubles place each player in the location where he will be able to capitalize most effectively on shots that come his way. The positions are advantageous for partners, and options are open depending on which type of strategy they wish to use.

THE PARALLEL THEORY

This is a theory whereby doubles partners play parallel to each other. They are responsible for covering all action in their respective halves of the court. Thus, their area of responsibility is from the center service line to the doubles sideline, on their side from the baseline to the net. Often players feel they are responsible for "all the net" or "all the baseline." This would dictate an up and back position and would leave too much area open. In good doubles play, both players are "up and back" frequently, but always play parallel to each other.

In the diagram we see the basic positions for doubles. The server (S) stands about three feet to the right of the center mark. The partner of the server (SP) stands in the left service court, about four feet from the singles sideline and about six to eight feet from the net. The receiver (R) stands at the baseline awaiting the service. R should bisect the angle of the service. The receiver's partner (RP) stands on the service line. These basic positions are used to begin each point. From here the initial strategy begins and will be dependent upon the knowledge and stroke production of the players involved. As the service is made, the server moves up into the court, trying to get as close to the net as possible before the receiver returns the ball. Usually a step inside the service line is all that can be achieved, but this depends upon the service and the speed of the server. As the service return passes over the net, the server uses a half-volley or a volley and progresses on in to establish a true net position. At this point he/she is alongside his/

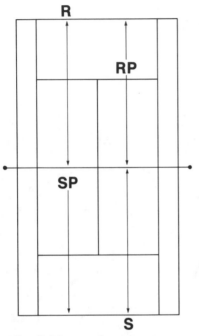

Parallel theory of court coverage (doubles)

her partner, generally parallel to the net. Usually the receiver (R) will also move toward the net after the service is returned. The receiver's partner (RP) is stepping toward the net in an effort to cut off the volley. Thus, we are frequently confronted with all 4 players at the net, looking for an opening to force an error or to hit a winner.

AUSTRALIAN DOUBLES

This method of play changes the formation most generally used in doubles play.

The RP is located as explained above. The SP now places himself in the service court in front of the *receiving net player.* The server, upon delivering the service, must now assume total responsibility for the returns coming "down the line" rather than cross court. The Aussie innovation will disturb those players accustomed to standard formations but will not make a difference to good players. See figures for the court positions used in Australian doubles.

POINTS OF INTEREST IN AUSTRALIAN DOUBLES

1. It is seldom used in good competition.
2. It protects against a sharp crosscourt service return.
3. The receiver usually can easily return down the line.
4. The server must cover the alley frequently, thus eliminating the approach to the net.
5. The surprise element is good on occasion if not overused.

CLUB OR "RECREATIONAL" DOUBLES

This style of play is presently worldwide in scope. It is primarily recreational in nature, and is played for fun. However, the competitive instincts are still used and the desire to win is sometimes intense.

In club doubles, we frequently find players who do not have the stroke production or the physical prowess to play aggressive "Basic"

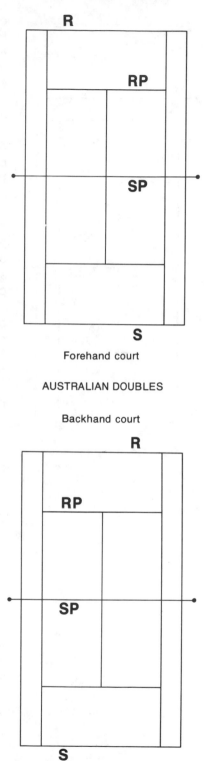

Forehand court

AUSTRALIAN DOUBLES

Backhand court

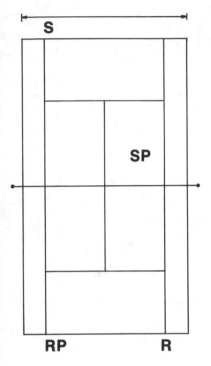

CLUB DOUBLES

competitive doubles. In many instances the footwork and hustle needed to get to the net is just not a part of the player. Also, trying to follow a somewhat weak serve to the net would be foolish.

Thus, we find that many players tend to play a formation of one-up, one-back. While this does not resemble two players in the center of the court in an "I" formation, it does have the basic characteristics of good doubles even though neither the server nor the receiver makes any attempt to go to the net. Play is frequently between the server and receiver only, with an occasional lob causing the players to "switch" sides, only to continue this basic style. It is very popular, comfortable, fun, and within the general capabilities of most players.

Of course, both players may stand anywhere on the court. This is sometimes seen in both players' staying on the baseline, keeping the ball going back and forth using crosscourt drives and down the line shots.

The "Club" style of play requires certain basic responsibilities:

1. Service to the weaker side of an opponent and deep into the service court.
2. Keep the ball in play.
3. Keep your return away from the net player.
4. If you lob, tell your partner.
5. If playing backcourt when your partner is at the net, cover lobs that go over his head. In other words, "switch" sides of court.
6. Don't poach unless you can win the point.

By playing together frequently, teammates can easily compliment each other, developing consistent placements, strategic volleys and accurate lobs. Then the team becomes hard to defeat.

TENNIS STRATEGY FOR DOUBLES

Good doubles is based upon the server's being able to hold serve. That is, to win the game you are serving. To do this requires proper placement, spin and speed on the serve. Remember, it only takes one service break to win or lose a set.

Doubles strategy demands that the best server on your team should serve first. This is because you will have an easier time holding service with your stronger server. The server should consider the following points when serving:

a. Determine which side (forehand or backhand) your opponent has the most difficulty with in returning serve, then attack that side. This is generally the backhand side!

b. Which serve gives the receiver more trouble? Slice, twist, flat? Go for that one frequently.

c. Look for an opening in the position of the receiver. This will create a weak return.

d. Keep enough speed on your serve to keep the receiver deep and protect your partner at the net.

e. Aim at the corners frequently to force a weak return.

f. Come to the net as often as you can.

g. Use variety in your serve. Don't allow the opponent to anticipate your serve with regularity. Mix them up.

h. Take your time on your serve.

i. Get your first serve in. It gives your team a great psychological advantage and your opponent will be deeper in his backcourt than on the second serve.

j. Use lots of spin on your second serve, but keep the opponent deep.

k. Let your partner know that he should try for any ball within his reach. Do poach whenever feasible.

l. Determine which player is the weaker, and play most of your shots to this opponent.

m. Arrange hand signals with your net man so you will know what he plans to do. Example — to poach or stay.

STRATEGY WHEN RECEIVING

Receiving service is just as important as serving. If you have a good return of service you can break the opponents' serve and win a game. This takes a lot of practice and should become one of your most sound strokes.

As in serving, returning the serve should be done with planning, care and deception. Using variety is important, but not to the point that careless errors become rampant in your game. Follow these guidelines as you think about your service returns:

a. Use variety, but with discretion.
b. Except when lobbing, keep your return low and wide to the feet of the net rusher.
c. If the opponent doesn't follow his serve to the net, return deep to the corner and go to the net.
d. Keep your return away from the net man.
e. Use the lob to throw the opponents off balance.
f. Get in as close as possible on the second serve as this gives the opponent less time to approach the net.
g. Learn to chip the return and come to the net.

Remember that your partner is moving up on your service return. If you are missing shots, check your fundamentals: footwork, eye on the ball, turning the side, and good stroke production. Stay with basic tennis strategy. Rarely vary from it.

USE OF THE VOLLEY, SMASH AND LOB

In doubles, the basic strategy of the game emphasizes the importance of net play. The initial alignment of players both in serving and receiving indicates a strong emphasis toward establishing an attack position at the net — thus, the volley, the smash and the lob become most important. If you are attempting to get to the net, the volley and/or the lob will assist you. Also, once there, the overhead smash will help you.

Let's briefly review the use of these three strokes as they pertain to basic doubles strategy.

The volley. Remember this stroke is used as an offensive weapon, attempting to win the point by an angle, or to force a weak return. On the serving side, the server's partner is already established at the net, hoping to cut off a drive and win the point. The server will serve and come to the net, often using the volley to get there. Once at the net, the volley will be used to assist in winning the point. The receiving team is also positioned to take the net position if the serving team doesn't beat them to it! The receiver's partner is at the service line ready to come in, and the receiver, if the server doesn't come in, should return deep and approach the net. The volley is the basic point winner in good doubles, as both players are at the net.

The smash. Of course, you had rather use the smash than the volley, because you will win the point quicker and more often. However, to use a smash, one needs to have an opponent send a lob that is short enough for smash execution. This can usually be done by a forcing ground stroke, service, or volley. Since everyone will be playing at the net, all doubles participants should have a good overhead.

The lob. This is the most unused shot in tennis. It is as though you are degrading yourself to use it. However, if executed properly it can be devastating to any tennis player. In doubles, you know that the opponents will be attacking the net position, this makes them vulnerable to the lob. Proper use of the lob will cause them to be pushed back from the attack position to a defensive position at the baseline. Also, if your lob is to their backhand, and has some topspin, you can easily attack behind this shot. So practice lobbing and enjoy the problems you give your opponents.

As seen in this chapter, doubles is a great game. Unlike singles, teamwork is involved. Good players complement each other. However, partners must know basic strategy and have good execution of fundamentals. You must understand what is expected of you insofar as serving, receiving, net play, court coverage and teamwork. Once you really "get into the game," you'll find great enjoyment in this new found challenge.

CHAPTER 12 EVALUATION

1. Discuss the parallel theory used in doubles play.

2. What are the advantages and disadvantages of "Australian Doubles"? How would you attack this system of play?

3. What are the weaknesses of "one up one back" doubles play?

4. How important is the volley in doubles play?

5. List several points of doubles strategy.

6. Discuss the role of the server in doubles play.

CHAPTER 13

CONDITIONING FOR TENNIS

THE IMPORTANCE OF THE WARM-UP

Tennis players do not warm up properly! It is hard to find a reason for this attitude. It may be that the process takes too much time or is more personal in that the players involved just feel they don't need it. Try to imagine this situation. You and your friend meet at the court for a match. You go to opposite sides of the court and begin hitting groundstrokes to each other. This continues for about ten minutes, then you take turns at the net for volleys and overheads, hit a few more "groundies," and start eight to ten practice serves. Enough of these and you're ready to play — right? WRONG!

All this warm-up time you have spent on stroking, timing and loosening up the racket arm. You've done very little to get the trunk, shoulders, and legs ready. Yet, on the first serve you are expected to go 100% into the game. There is no way you can be ready for the stress you may demand. Have you ever watched a sprinter go through a warm-up? This will show the care one should take in exercising the entire body.

Your warm-up should include calisthenics, mild jogging, stretching exercises, flexibility and agility movements BEFORE you get on the court. This should take from 10-20 minutes if you plan your time and program wisely. Isolate yourself from the group, club, or court if you wish and go through your pre-planned workout by yourself. Don't be self-conscious. If your friends see you, they will only realize that you are the smarter person. Upon completion, take a few minutes to relax. Then walk to your court. You will find that you are mentally and

psychologically ready for the match, and you can go after any shot your opponent hits without fear of a strain or muscle tear. Also, if you plan it right, you will stand a very good chance of breaking service early, simply because you are better prepared early in the match. You won't need to warm up as the set gets underway.

CONDITIONING EXERCISES

CONDITIONING PROGRAMS

Several types of programs can be used for conditioning the body. You may select a program of calisthenics, circuit training, weight training, or one primarily of running and light stretching type exercises. Following is a brief explanation of these programs.

A. **Calisthenics** — light gymnastics type exercises generally done without the use of equipment. They are useful in the development of flexibility, strength and endurance, and are beneficial as a warm-up activity. Examples are the cross-leg stretch, push-ups, bent knee sit-ups, burpee, half squat, raise on toes, rowing and running in place. There are hundreds of beneficial exercises of this type. Select those which you feel will compliment your program.

B. **Circuit training** — a fitness program of carefully selected exercises arranged in stations. They are numbered consecutively

Push-ups

Hurdler's stretch

Sprinting

Leg and groin stretch

Toe touch

and in a limited area. The purpose of circuit training exercises is to improve muscular strength and endurance, improve flexibility and to improve the cardiovascular and respiratory endurance. It is reasonable to realize that various items of equipment will be needed at some stations. An example of a circuit training program is listed below.

STATION	EXERCISES
1	Isometrics 6 sec. X 3 reps.
2	Squat Balance — 10 sec.
3	Inverted Bicycle — 100 count
4	"Cat Stretch" — 1 min.
5.	Hurdler Stretch — 30 sec. each leg
6	Run in Place — 1 min.
7	Body Stretch — 15 reps.
8	Isometrics — 6 sec. X 4
9	Isometrics — 6 sec. X 4
10	Double Rowing — 1 min.
11	Knee lift — 15 reps.
12	Squat Jumps — 30 reps.
13	Wrist roller — 2 ea. reg. and reverse
14	"V" position — 60 sec.
15	Hand Walk — Parallel Bars X 3
16	Rope skipping — 1 min.
17	Sit Ups — Bent knee — 1 min.
18	Dips — max. effort
19	Cross leg stretch — 15R, 15L
20	Pull ups — max. effort

Hamstring stretch

Sit-ups

This may be shortened to suit the individual concerned. Specific exercises may be selected depending on the goals and purposes of the player. This program is frequently combined with speed and distance running to achieve the maximum benefit.

C. **Weight training** — a program specifically designed for the development of muscular strength and muscular endurance. It is probably the best of all exercise programs for the development of strength, and combines well with a program of aerobics for a high degree of all around fitness. Individuals should decide whether their prime purpose is to develop muscular strength or muscular endurance, since the amount of resistance, the number of sets, and the number of repetitions will vary with the purpose.

A proper program of weight training will combine exercises or routines that strengthen every part of the body used in tennis — the forearms, wrists, shoulders, back, abdomen, thighs, legs, and ankles. Once you establish the types of routines you want, begin with light weights and progress slowly into the overload principle until you reach the level you desire. Follow general safety rules of weight training, and don't try to take short cuts, as an injury may result.

Competitive tennis places heavy demands on the ankles, abdominal areas, shoulders and thighs. Proper selection will demand emphasis on these areas. A regularly scheduled workout, combined with adequate aerobic activity, three times a week is preferable in the off-season months. Begin to taper off as the season approaches utilizing only "maintenance" workout when intense competition begins.

Before beginning your training program be sure to clear your plans with a physician. Select proper clothing and shoes for running and find a place away from traffic and other nuisances. You also will be wise to stay away from hard surfaced areas like streets, sidewalks and bike paths. These surfaces tend to place too much strain on critical joints and will also cause shin splints, a very painful ailment occurring in the lower legs. Other problems with street running are heavy traffic, undue concentrations of carbon monoxide gas, and the danger of being struck by a vehicle.

You will find that running, supplemented with other exercise routines, will greatly benefit your tennis game. An added extra, such as rope jumping, will also contribute greatly to endurance, and your footwork will also begin to improve. It will soon be noticeable that you are getting to the ball more quickly, and your entire game will improve. Most importantly you will begin to develop more confidence in yourself and your game.

D. **Running** — It is most beneficial to develop the heart and lungs — the cardio-vascular and cardio-pulmonary systems within the body. When one speaks of being "in shape" the question becomes "in shape for what?" If being a serious tennis player is important to you, then serious running is necessary to develop the cardio-vascular and cardio-pulmonary systems.

The various programs mentioned earlier are good, and will contribute greatly to various parts of your conditioning. Certainly you will need all the components of fitness: speed, agility, flexibility, muscular strength and muscular endurance, balance and power, to mention several important areas. However, a large percentage of your fitness training should be directed toward cardiovascular endurance. That is, to train the heart and lungs to the point that you will not tire during a long three-set match, as endurance often makes the difference between success and failure.

How much running is necessary? Generally speaking, from fifteen to twenty-five minutes a day about three to five times per week should be sufficient. It is important to begin slowly and progress upward to two miles or more. Many tennis players in the collegiate ranks are now running three to five miles daily, and enjoying their workouts!

CHAPTER 13 EVALUATION

1. Explain your attitude towards the warm-up as you have always taken it.

2. What elements should a proper warm-up include? What time-factor is involved?

3. There are many conditioning programs that are available to almost everyone. Which style will fit your NEEDS best? Remember, it is not just "how much time do I have" but "how much time should I spend?"

4. List some of the basic benefits of weight training. Would your program be one of muscle strength or endurance? or both? How will you accomplish this goal?

CHAPTER 14

PRACTICE DRILLS

Tennis drills should be progressive in nature. There are no shortcuts in learning skill patterns. A student of the game should first seek professional instruction which will set the pace, determine the course, and generate interest in achieving one's potential. The tennis instructor should then establish drills and patterns for practice. Many of these drills will be "dry" drills using no balls, but simply going through the stroking pattern to learn the sequence and to train the muscles in acquiring the new skill.

Practically speaking, drills are divided into four general areas. These are:
a. Footwork drills
b. Basic instructional drills
c. Intermediate skill drills
d. Advanced competitive drills

Each group is divided into many individual drills that are progressive in nature, and easy to understand.

SELECTED FOOTWORK DRILLS

It has been said, and reliably so, that footwork is about 60% of the game of tennis. This being the case, it becomes obvious that this fundamental must be developed to the maximum level. Each serious student of the game should have a practice plan which will achieve maximum results. The following footwork patterns have been selected because of their aggressiveness, practicality, and conditioning benefits. No balls are actually hit in any of these footwork drills.

Jump rope. Using primarily a single hop. May be done on both feet, or either one. Can be very useful also as a conditioner. There are several patterns and styles that can be used.

Crossover step. Punch volley each step. Begin in a ready position then use a cross-step (forward pivot) to the forehand and to the backhand in quick repetition, hitting an imaginary volley each time. Emphasis is on speed and correct footwork pattern. Do four to six thirty-second rounds.

Serve and go. Begin at the baseline, without use of tennis balls, serve and go to the net, using a check-stop at the service line, continue to the net. Repeat many times.

Zig zag run. From center mark, place balls in an irregular pattern on either side. Using a broken pattern proceed to each ball on the ground and stroke each imaginary ball at the location of the ball on the ground.

Up the alley. Using the cross-step pattern mentioned in #2 above, begin at the baseline on one side of the alley. Use the pattern to cross and punch an imaginary volley, continuing to move forward each step. Continue until you go "up the alley." Execution should be rapid and the footwork should be correct. Do approximately six rounds.

Up and over. Start at the singles sideline. Begin by moving forward to the service line then stop and hit an imaginary groundstroke, then go along the service line to the midcourt line, stop and hit a groundstroke, go up the midcourt line to the net, punch a volley, then go the side — right or left — and extend (stretch) to hit the final volley. Go to the opposite side of the baseline and begin again. Go through five times.

Side step drill. Place yourself halfway between the midcourt line and singles sideline. Using a side skipping motion, move to a point that will allow you to stroke a ball at the singles sideline, pivot and stroke. Then rapidly recover and move to the midcourt line and execute a stroke, repeat for 30 seconds. Then start again. Continue for four to six repetitions.

Jog and stroke. Starting at court #1 on your court complex, begin to jog around the courts. Check stop every five steps and stroke a forehand or a backhand, alternating with each stop. Continue around the courts.

Shuttle run. Place four balls on the court equidistant from the baseline to the net. Begin by running, racket in hand, to the first ball, return to the baseline running backwards, then go to the second ball. Continue to the baseline backwards, then on to the third, etc., until you go to all four balls. Repeat three times.

Quick step and volley. Spread out on the court. Begin running in place. On every tenth step quickly execute a forehand volley, recover and continue to run in place, then a backhand volley is hit. Continue this routine for thirty seconds or more. This can be done easily with a partner using hand signals — you move to the side according to the partner's lifting his right or left arm quickly. Be alert. Continue to move the feet at all times.

BASIC INSTRUCTIONAL DRILLS

THE FOREHAND	REPETITIONS

1. From a ready position, obtain the "shake hands" grip. Release, repeat.   10
2. From a ready position, try the forward pivot, check foot position, recover.   10
3. Repeat No. 2 above using the reverse pivot.   10
4. Using the forward pivot, take the complete backswing. Check height of the racket hand.   10
5. Using the forward pivot, combine the backswing, forward swing and follow-through in one smooth, flowing motion.   10
6. From the back of the court, turn your left side to the fence. Drop a ball in *front* of the left side and stroke the ball into the fence twenty feet away. Recover to ready position, then repeat. Now hit ball over the net.   25
7. Drop a ball as in #6 and stroke it to a rebound wall. Catch ball, drop and repeat.   25
8. Repeat #7, keeping the ball to the right half of the forward rebound wall and above the three-foot net line.   20
9. Repeat #8, keeping the ball in play to the right half of the forward rebound wall.   20
10. Try to replay the rebound against the forward wall. (number of bounces is not important at this stage)   30

PARTNER DRILLS	REPETITIONS

11. Have a partner toss from the net (center) to a circle just behind the service line. Stroke using full pivot.   30
12. Toss from net into a circle just above the baseline, stroke from baseline into opponent's court. Use full pivot.   30
13. Repeat #12, except substitute a ball machine for tosser. Hit three baskets of balls apiece.   3
14. Repeat #13. Aim each ball to the opposite side of opponent's court from the last ball. (check fundamentals)   3
15. Drop a ball and stroke to your partner on the opposite side of the net. Try to continue a forehand rally.   30 minutes

If you detect any trouble with the forehand, go back and review the fundamentals. Acquire a good *mental picture* of what you are after. If you *understand* it, it will greatly assist you in skill development.

THE BACKHAND

As in the forehand, the drills listed below are in progressive order from the simple to the complex. If you use these drills, take your time and go slowly. The number of repetitions are used as a guide only. You may need fewer, or more, depending on your particular progress.

BACKHAND   REPETITIONS

1. From a ready position, change from a forehand grip to a backhand grip.   10
2. Repeat #1, and use the forward pivot to the left side changing grips as you execute the pivot. Check footwork positions.   10
3. Repeat #2, only use the reverse pivot, stepping back rather than forward.   10
4. Using the forward pivot, take the racket back in to the full backswing position. Check height of racket head (keep low).   10
5. Repeat #4, and add the forward swing and follow-through. Go very slowly, check racket head position. Lead with the head of racket.   15
6. From the back of the court area turn the right side to the fence, drop a ball in front of the right side and execute a backhand stroke to the fence, twenty feet away. Recover, and repeat.   25
7. Drop a ball and stroke it to a rebound wall. Catch the ball and repeat.   25
8. Repeat #7, except aim the ball above an imaginary three-foot line representing the tennis net.   25
9. Repeat #8, keeping the ball to the left side of the front wall.   20
10. Try to replay the rebound against the forward wall. (number of bounces is not important now)   30

PARTNER DRILLS   REPETITIONS

11. Have a partner toss from the center of the net into a small circle behind service line. Stroke using a full backhand stroke with pivot, adjusting the toss to the circle.   30
12. Toss from the net into a circle just above the baseline. Stroke from baseline into opponent's court. Use full pivot.   30
13. Repeat #12, except substitute ball machine for tosser. Hit at least three trays of balls each.   3+
14. Repeat #13, aim each ball to the opposite side of opponent's court from the last ball. Check your fundamentals.   3
15. Drop a ball and stroke to your partner on the opposite side of the net. Try to continue a backhand rally.   30 minutes

16. Using both forehand and backhand, drop a ball and keep a rally going as long as possible. Continue until your continuous count totals 1,000 shots hit over the net.

You have now completed the two basic strokes in tennis. If there is a problem you cannot handle, contact your instructor, or go back and read and repeat your skill progressions. When you have completed the work on the backhand stroke, review the skill and knowledge objectives to determine if further emphasis is needed.

THE SERVICE	REPETITIONS
1. Practice the coordination of swing for both arms. Right arm to backswing and left arm toward ball toss. Shift weight back as arms begin movement. DO NOT TOSS BALL.	20
2. Practice the toss of the ball. Noticing the height, and where it lands on the court.	30
3. Repeat #1, toss ball up as racket arm is taken back. Do not hit the ball.	25
4. Repeat #3. Face the fence, and serve into the fence, work on ball toss, contact point, and height.	30
5. At service line, serve five good serves diagonally across to correct service court.	5
6. Repeat #5, except move back one yard after each five good serves, gradually working your way to the baseline.	5+
7. *From the baseline,* using the correct form, serve ten to right court, then ten to left court. Repeat.	20+
8. Serve 20 flat serves into the right service court.	
9. Serve 20 flat serves into the left service court.	
10. Serve 100 balls to each service court. R + L.	200
11. Divide the opposite service courts into quarters. Serve 25 balls to each area.	
Area #1 — Forehand corner for receiver — *Right service court*	25
Area #2 — Backhand corner for receiver — *Right service court*	25
Area #3 — Forehand corner for receiver — *Left service court*	25
Area #4 — Backhand corner for receiver — *Left service court*	25

As you continue to practice, aim the ball to either area 1 or 2, or area 3 or 4, depending on which side you are serving from. Remember to always serve *diagonally across* the court.

12. Repeat #10, but serve 50 serves to each area (one
through four) in numerical order.   200

Increase your speed only as you are able to maintain control and
placement.

THE VOLLEY   REPETITIONS

1. From proper net position, have partner toss balls to
your forehand, from service line. Volley back to your
partner. Keep toss chest high, toss overhand.   30
2. Repeat #1, except now use the backhand volley.   30
3. Alternate forehand and backhand volley, hit from toss
back to partner. Toss overhand.   50
4. Forehand only, vary height of the toss. Direct volley
toward partner if possible.   50
5. Repeat #4 using the backhand.   30
6. Repeat #3, aim ball to opposite corner of opponent's
court.   30
7. Repeat #3, aim ball to opposite corner of opponent's
court.   30
8. Using a ball machine, alternate loads to the forehand
and backhand, two rounds of balls to each side.   4
9. Using the machine, from the same tossing position
move from the base line, stroking the ball to the
opponent's backhand, then as you move to the net,
volley the next ball. (Repeat: 10 approach shots and 10
volleys.)   20
10. Have baseline partner, stroke a ball to you at the net,
then volley the ball back to partner for another ground
stroke. Feed the ball to each other.   20

THE SMASH   REPETITIONS

1. Obtain the correct grip, turn the left side to the net in
the forecourt area, and execute the full swing without a
ball.   10
2. Toss from the baseline to the partner at the net
(forecourt). Smash the ball at half speed into the
opponent's court.
3. Repeat #2, but begin aiming the ball at different
angles (left, right, short, deep.)   30
4. Repeat #2, but aim the ball to the opponent's deep
backcourt area.   20
5. Have partner lob the ball to you with his racket.
Execute the smash to varying areas of opponent's
courts.   20

SKILL DRILLS

Most skill drills are part of an intensive practice plan. There are drills for each stroke often using a partner to feed the ball. There are three drill areas that are basic to good tennis and should be practiced on a regular basis. These areas are:

    a. Serve and return of serve

    b. Groundstroke consistency and accuracy from the baseline

    c. Placement of passing shots

Also, additional time should be given to the accomplishment of the support strokes, or those which compliment the basic game. These areas are:

    a. Combination of serve and volley

    b. Use of the approach shot

    c. The volley and net tactics

    d. The overhead or smash

    e. Offensive and defensive lobs

Time should be allowed for practice and play, with neither partner totally dominating the other. Some selected skill drills are as follows.

1. Rally from the back court area at the center mark.
2. Stroke crosscourt shots — both backhand and forehand rallies.
3. Use an "X" drill. One partner hits crosscourt only while the other partner hits down the line only.
4. Two partners face each other near the sideline. One hits forehand down the line and the partner hits backhands. They hit to each other.
5. One partner has basket of balls at service line. Hit balls to partner running partner from corner to corner.
6. Serve only — to both forehand and backhand service courts.
7. One at the net, one at baseline — rally.
8. Same as #7, using only forehand or only backhand.
9. One at net, one at baseline, volley and lob practice.
10. Using a feeder, hit forehand or backhand volleys only.
11. Overheads, feed setups from the baseline.
12. Volley-rally-overhead drill.
13. Hit overhead, touch net, hit overhead, and touch net, continue 10 times.
14. Four-ball drill, hit from baseline, half-volley at service line, volley at net and overhead.
15. Serve and lob return drill.
16. Serve or return serve to target area.
17. Angled volley to backhand cones — either side.
18. Both partners at net — volley.
19. Same as #18 only use crosscourt volley.
20. Volley rally against a wall.

COMPETITIVE DRILLS

These drills may use a point system to encourage a "game-like" situation. Practice should be intense and care taken not to make careless errors. Most are aggressive and demand skill competency.

1. Serve and return of serve.
2. Serve and play out point.
3. Serve and follow serve to net (use check-stop).
4. Serve or go to net — service return cannot bounce on server's side.
5. Serve — only one service per point — and play point.
6. Volley — two at the net — slow to fast — use point system.
7. Volley — to baseline rally — try to pass opponent at net.
8. Volley — only to forehand or backhand side. Try to pass. Volley goes down the line only.
9. Volley — four at the net — keep one ball going.
10. Two vs one at the baseline. One tries to pass two at net.
11. Two vs one at the net. Two try to pass one at the net.
12. Protect your partner — doubles set up — use rally — attempt to poach.
13. Serve and lob return to backhand quarter of court.
14. Return serve to target area on court.
15. Serve to target on service court.
16. Depth rally — hit to backcourt area only — use point system.
17. Long rally — count number of hits between partners — try for best score — one bounce.
18. Consecutive volleys from inside service line. Count score.
19. Volley rally vs rebound wall. Number of volleys in one minute.
20. "King of the Court." Singles. Play first to reach 10 points, rotate serve. Winner moves one court toward #1 court, loser stays. Loser on #1 goes to bottom and starts over (singles and doubles).
21. Halfcourt game of 21 — lengthwise. All shots must be within 1/2 court area. Putaway smash = 3 points, volley = 2 points. All others = 1 point. Rotate serve each 5 points.
22. Lob rally — 4 players — 2 deep, 2 at net within service line. Net men put away all short lobs.
23. Four ball drill X five times. Count number of balls in the court.
24. Short game using service courts only.

CHAPTER 14 EVALUATION

1. List and diagram two individual drills for each of the following: forehand, backhand, service, volley, and lob.

2. List and diagram two "partner drills" for the above shots.

3. What is "progression" and how important is it to the development of skill proficiency?

CHAPTER 15

UNABRIDGED RULES OF TENNIS

*Reprinted by permission of USTA.

EXPLANATORY NOTE

The appended Code of Rules and Cases and Decisions is the Official Code of the International Tennis Federation, of which the United States Tennis Association is a member.

Italicized EXPLANATIONS, EXAMPLES, NOTES and COMMENTS have been prepared by the USTA Rules Interpretation Committee to amplify and facilitate interpretation of the formal code.

SPECIAL NOTE: In July, 1978 the ITF adopted several new rules and made changes in several others. Most notable were the adoption of a new Rule (No. 4) defining the racket; the setting of new time limits between points and on changeovers (in what now is Rule 31), and adoption of a no-coaching Rule (No. 32). Therefore the numeration of almost all the rules has been altered. In this printing the added or changed material appears in bold-face type.

THE SINGLES GAME

RULE 1

Dimensions and Equipment

The court shall be a rectangle 78 feet (23.77m) long and 27 feet (8.23m) wide. It shall be divided across the middle by a net suspended from a cord or metal cable of a maximum diameter of one-third of an inch (0.8cm), the ends of which shall be attached to, or pass over, the tops of two posts, 3 feet 6 inches (1.07m) high, and not more than 6 inches (15cm) in diameter, the centers of which shall be 3 feet (0.91m) outside the court on each side. The net shall be extended fully so that it fills completely the space between the two posts and shall be of sufficiently small mesh to prevent the ball's passing through. The height of the net shall be 3 feet (0.914m) at the center, where it shall be held down taut by a strap not more than 2 inches (5cm) wide and white in color. There shall be a band covering the cord or metal cable and the top of the net for not less than 2 inches (5cm) nor more than 2½ inches (6.3cm) in depth on each side and white in color. There shall be no advertisement on the net, strap, band or singles sticks. The lines bounding the ends and sides of the Court shall respectively be called the Baselines and the Sidelines. On each side of the net, at a distance of 21 feet (6.40m) from it and parallel with it, shall be drawn the Service lines. The space on each side of the net between the service line and the sidelines shall be divided into two equal parts, called the service courts, by the center service line, which must be 2 inches (5cm) in width, drawn half-way between, and parallel with, the sidelines. Each baseline shall be bisected by an imaginary continuation of the center service line to a line 4 inches (10cm) in length and 2 inches (5cm) in width called the center mark, drawn inside the Court at right angles to and in contact with such baselines. All other lines shall be not less than 1 inch (2.5cm) nor more than 2 inches (5cm) in width, except the baseline, which may be 4 inches (10cm) in width, and all measurements shall be made to the outside of the lines.

Note — In the case of the International Tennis Championship (Davis Cup) or other Official Championships of the International Federation, there shall be a space behind each baseline of not less than 21 feet (6.4m), and at the sides of not less than 12 feet (3.66m).

The center of the posts in doubles should be 3 feet outside the doubles court.

The net should be 33 feet in the clear for a singles court, and 42 feet wide for a doubles court. The net should touch the ground along its entire length and come flush to the posts at all points.

It is important to have a stick 3 feet, 6 inches long, with a notch cut in at the 3-foot mark for the purpose of measuring the height of the net at the posts and in the center. These measurements always should be made before starting to play a match. When a singles match is to be played with a doubles net in place, a singles stick should be placed 36 inches outside each sideline to make the net 42 inches high at those points.

RULE 2

Permanent Fixtures

The permanent fixtures of the Court shall include not only the net, posts, cord or metal cable, strap and band, but also, where there are any such, the back and side stops, the stands, fixed or movable seats and chairs around the Court, and their occupants, all other fixtures around and above the Court, and the Chair Umpire, Net Umpire, Line Umpires and Ball Boys when in their respective places.

DIAGRAM AND DIMENSIONS OF TENNIS COURT

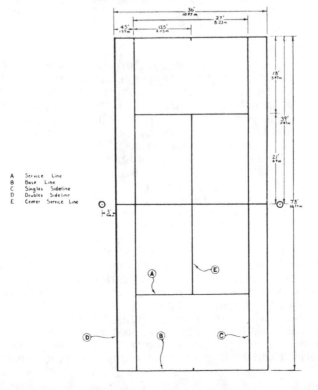

A   Service Line
B   Base Line
C   Singles Sideline
D   Doubles Sideline
E   Center Service Line

RULE 3

Ball — Size, Weight and Bound

The ball shall have a uniform outer surface and shall be white or yellow in color. If there are any seams they shall be stitchless. The ball shall be more than two and a half inches (6.35cm) and less than two and five-eighths inches (6.67cm) in diameter, and more than two ounces (56.7 grams) and less than two and one-sixteenth ounces (58.5 grams) in weight. The ball shall have a bound of more than 53 inches (135cm) and less than 58 inches (147cm) when dropped 100 inches (254cm) upon a concrete base. The ball shall have a forward deformation of more than .220 of an inch (.56cm) and less than .290 of an inch (.74cm) and a return deformation of more than .350 of an inch (.89cm) and less than .425 of an inch (1.08cm) at 18 lbs. (8.165 kg) load. The two deformation figures shall be the averages of three individual readings along three axes of the ball and no two individual readings shall differ by more than .030 of an inch (.08cm) in each case. Regulations for conducting tests for bound, size and deformation of balls may be found in the Appendix hereto.

Note — At the Annual General Meeting of the ITF held on 12th July, 1967, it was agreed that for the time being non-pressurized balls and low-pressure balls may not be used in the International Tennis Championship (Davis Cup), unless mutually agreed by the two nations taking part in any particular event.

NOTE
"How often may the player have new balls?"
The ball-change pattern is specified by the Referee before the match is started. According to Tournament Regulations the Chair Umpire may call for a ball change at other than the prescribed time when in his opinion abnormal conditions warrant so doing. In a non-officiated match the players should agree beforehand on this matter.

RULE 4

The Racket

The racket shall consist of a frame and a stringing. The frame may be of any material, weight, size or shape.

The strings must be alternately interlaced or bonded where they cross, and each string must be connected to the frame. If there are attachments, they must be used only to prevent wear and tear and must not alter the flight of the ball. The density in the center must be at least equal to the average density of the stringing. The stringing must be made so that the moves between the strings will not exceed that which is possible, for instance, with 18 mains and 18 crosses uniformly spaced and interlaced in a stringing area of 75 square inches.

Note — The spirit of this rule is to prevent undue spin on the ball that would result in a change in the character of the game.

RULE 5

Server and Receiver

The Players shall stand on opposite side of the net; the player who first delivers the ball shall be called the Server, and the other the Receiver.

Case 1. Does a player, attempting a stroke, lose the point if he crosses an imaginary line in the extension of the net, (a) before striking the ball (b) after striking the ball?
Decision. He does not lose the point in either case by crossing the imaginary line provided he does not enter the lines bounding his opponent's court. (Rule 20 (e.) In regard to hindrance, his opponent may ask for the decision of the umpire under Rules 21 and 25.

Case 2. The Server claims that the Receiver must stand within the lines bounding his court. Is this necessary?

Decision: No. The Receiver may stand wherever he pleases on his own side of the net.

RULE 6

Choice of Ends and Service

The choice of ends and the right to be Server or Receiver in the first game shall be decided by toss. The player winning the toss may choose, or require his opponent to choose:

(a) The right to be Server or Receiver, in which case the other player shall choose the end; or

(b) The end, in which case the other player shall choose the right to be Server or Receiver.

NOTE – These choices should be made promptly, and are irrevocable.

RULE 7

Delivery of Service

The service shall be delivered in the following manner. Immediately before commencing to serve, the Server shall stand with both feet at rest behind (i.e. farther from the net than) the base-line, and within the imaginary continuations of the center-mark and side-line. The Server shall then project the ball by hand into the air in any direction and before it hits the ground strike it with his racket, and the delivery shall be deemed to have been completed at the moment of the impact of the racket and the ball. A player with the use of only one arm may utilize his racket for the projection.

Case 1. May the Server in a singles game take his stand behind the portion of the base-line between the sidelines of the singles court and the doubles court?

Decision. No.

Case 2. If a player, when serving, throws up two or more balls instead of one, does he lose that service?

Decision. No. A let should be called, but if the umpire regards the action as deliberate he may take action under Rule 21.

Case 3. May a player serve underhand?

Decision. Yes. There is no restriction regarding the kind of service which may be used; that is, the player may use an underhand or overhand service at his discretion.

RULE 8

Foot Fault

The Server shall throughout the delivery of the service:

(a) Not change his position by walking or running.

(b) Not touch, with either foot, any area other than that behind the base-line within the imaginary extension of the center-mark and side-line.

Note — The following interpretation of Rule 8 was approved by the International Federation on 9th July 1958: —

(a) The Server shall not, by slight movements of the feet which do not materially affect the location originally taken up by him, be deemed "to change his position by walking or running."

(b) The word "foot" means the extremity of the leg below the ankle.

COMMENT: This rule covers the most decisive stroke in the game, and there is no justification for its not being obeyed by players and enforced by officials. No tournament official has the right to request or attempt to instruct any umpires to disregard violations of it.

RULE 9

From Alternate Courts

(a) In delivering the service, the Server shall stand alternately behind the right and left Courts, beginning from the right in every game. If service from a wrong half of the Court occurs and is undetected, all play resulting from such wrong service or services shall stand, but the inaccuracy of the station shall be corrected immediately it is discovered.

(b) The ball served shall pass over the net and hit the ground within the Service Court which is diagonally opposite, or upon any line bounding such Court, before the Receiver returns it.

COMMENT: The Receiver is not allowed to volley a served ball, i.e., he must allow it to strike in his court first. (See Rule 18 (a).

NOTE: In matches played without umpires, it is customary for the Receiver to determine whether the service is good or a fault; indeed each player makes the calls for all balls hit to his side of the net. (In doubles, the Receiver's partner makes the calls with respect to the service line.) It is the prerogative of the Receiver, or his partner, to call a foot fault or faults, but only after all efforts (appeal to the server, requests for monitoring help, etc.) have failed, and the foot faulting is so flagrant as to be clearly perceptible from the Receiver's side.

RULE 10

Faults

The Service is a fault:

(a) If the Server commit any breach of Rules 7, 8, or 9;

(b) If he miss the ball in attempting to strike it;

(c) If the ball served touch a permanent fixture (other than the net, strap or band) before it hits the ground.

Case 1. After throwing a ball up preparatory to serving, the Server decides not to strike at it and catches it instead. Is it a fault?

Decision. No.

Case 2. In serving in a singles game played on a doubles court with doubles and singles net posts, the ball hits a singles post and then hits the ground within the lines of the correct service court. Is this a fault or a let?

Decision. In serving it is a fault, because the singles post, the doubles post, and that portion of the net, strap or band between them are permanent fixtures. (Rules 2 and 10, and note to Rule 24.)

EXPLANATION: The significant point governing Case 2 is that the part of the net and band "outside" the singles sticks is not part of the net over which this singles match is being played. Thus such a serve is a fault under the provisions of Article (c) above . . . By the same token, this would be a fault also if it were a singles game played with permanent posts in the singles position. (See Case 1 under Rule 24 for difference between "service" and "good return" with respect to a ball's hitting a net post.)

COMMENT: In doubles, if the Server's delivery hits his partner, the serve is a fault (not necessarily loss of point). See Rule 40.

RULE 11

Service After a Fault

After a fault (if it be the first fault) the Server shall serve again from behind the same half of the Court from which he served that fault, unless the service was from the wrong half, when, in accordance with Rule 9, the Server shall be entitled to one service only from behind the other half. A fault may not be claimed after the next service has been delivered.

Case 1. A player serves from a wrong court. He loses the point and then claims it was a fault because of his wrong station.

Decision. The point stands as played and the next service should be from the correct station according to the score.

Case 2. The point score being 15 all, the Server, by mistake, serves from the left-hand court. He wins the point. He then serves again from the right-hand court, delivering a fault. The mistake in station is then discovered. Is he entitled to the previous point? From which court should be next serve?

Decision. The previous point stands. The next service should be from the left-hand court, the score being 30/15, and the Server has served one fault.

NOTE: When a first service is belatedly determined by the officials to have been a fault – either during the ensuing rally or after the point has been played out – the chair umpire is authorized to grant a full "let" (i.e. first service to come) on the ground of the nature and extent of the delay. Of course, if such belated call were on a second service the Server would lose the point.

RULE 12

Receiver Must Be Ready

The Server shall not serve until the Receiver is ready. If the latter attempts to return the service, he shall be deemed ready. If, however, the Receiver signify that he is not ready, he may not claim a fault because the ball does not hit the ground within the limits fixed for the service.

NOTE: The Server must wait until the Receiver is ready for the second service as well as the first, and if the Receiver claims to be not ready and does not make any effort to return a service, the Server may not claim the point, even though the service was good.

RULE 13

A Let

NOTE: A service that touches the net in passing yet falls into the proper court (or touches the receiver) is a let. This word is used also when, because of an interruption while the ball is in play, or for any other reason, a point is to be replayed.

In all cases where a let has to be called under the rules, or to provide for an interruption to play, it shall have the following interpretations:

(a) When called solely in respect of a service, that one service only shall be replayed.

(b) When called under any other circumstance, the point shall be replayed.

NOTE: A spectator's outcry (of "out," "fault" or other) is not a valid basis for replay of a point, but action should be taken to prevent a recurrence.

Case 1. A service is interrupted by some cause outside those defined in Rule 14. Should the service only be re-played?

Decision. No, the whole point must be replayed.

EXPLANATION: The phrase "in respect of a service" in (a) means a let because a served ball has touched the net before landing in the proper court, OR because the Receiver was not ready . . . Case 1 refers to a second serve, and the decision means that if the interruption occurs during delivery of the second service, the Server gets two serves.

EXAMPLE: On a second service a Linesman calls "fault" and immediately corrects it (the Receiver meanwhile having let the ball go by). The Server is entitled to two serves, on this ground: The corrected call means that the Server had put the ball into play with a good service, and once the ball is in play and a let is called, the point must be replayed . . . Note, however, that if the serve were an unmistakable ace – that is, the Umpire was sure the erroneous call had no part in the Receiver's inability to play the ball – the point should be declared for the Server.

Case 2. If a ball in play becomes broken, should a let be called?

Decision. Yes.

NOTE: A ball shall be regarded as having become "broken" if, in the opinion of the Chair Umpire, it is found to have lost compression to the point of being unfit for further play, or unfit for any reason, and it is clear the defective ball was the one in play.

RULE 14

The Service Is A Let

The service is a let:

(a) If the ball served touch the net, strap or band, is otherwise good, or, after touching the net, strap or band, touch the Receiver or anything which he wears or carries before hitting the ground. In case of such a let, that particular service does not count, and the Server shall serve again; but a service let does not annul a previous fault.

COMMENT: Also, a "let" called for the reason the Receiver had indicated he is not ready, on second service, does not annul a fault on first serve.

(b) If a service or a fault be delivered when the Receiver is not ready (see Rule 12).

RULE 15

When Receiver Becomes Server

At the end of the first game the Receiver shall become the Server, and the Server Receiver; and so on alternately in all the subsequent games of a match. If a player serve out of turn, the player who ought to have served shall serve as soon as the mistake is discovered, but all points scored before such discovery shall be reckoned. If a game shall have been completed before such discovery, the order of service remains as altered. A fault served before such discovery shall not be reckoned.

NOTE: If an error in serving sequence occurs and is discovered during a TIE-BREAKER game the serving sequence should be adjusted immediately so as to bring the number of points served by each player into the fairest possible balance. All completed points shall count.

RULE 16

When Players Change Ends

The players shall change ends at the end of the first, third and every subsequent alternate game of each set, and at the end of each set unless the total number of games in such set be even, in which case the change is not made until the end of the first game of the next set.

If a mistake is made and the correct sequence is not followed the players must take up their correct station as soon as the discovery is made and follow their original sequence.

EXPLANATION: If the mistake is discovered during a game the change in ends will be made at once, with all points that have been played counting, as a game. If the mistake is discovered at the end of a game, action that involves the smallest number of changes to get back to the original sequence of court occupancy, with an equitable division of games-per-end-per-player, should be taken.

RULE 17

Ball in Play Till Point Decided

A ball is in play from the moment at which it is delivered in service. Unless a fault or let be called, it remains in play until the point is decided.

COMMENT: A point is not "decided" simply when, or because, a good shot has clearly passed a player, nor when an apparently bad shot passes over a baseline or sideline. An outgoing ball is still definitely "in play" until it actually strikes the ground, backstop or a permanent fixture, or a player. The same applies to a good ball, bounding after it has landed in the proper court. A ball that becomes imbedded in the net is out of play.

Case 1. A ball is played into the net; the player on the other side, thinking that the ball is coming over, strikes at it and hits the net. Who loses the point?

Decision. If the player touched the net while the ball was still in play, he loses the point.

RULE 18

Server Wins Point

This Server wins the point:

(a) If the ball served, not being a let under Rule 14, touches the Receiver or anything which he wears or carries, before it hits the ground;
(b) If the Receiver otherwise loses the point as provided by Rule 20.

RULE 19

Receiver Wins Point

The Receiver wins the point:

(a) If the Server serve two consecutive faults;
(b) If the Server otherwise loses the point as provided by Rule 20.

RULE 20
(Formerly Rule 18)

Player Loses Point

A player loses the point if:

(a) He fail, before the ball in play has hit the ground twice consecutively, to return it directly over the net (except as provided in Rule 24 (a) or (c)); or
(b) He return the ball in play so that it hits the ground, a permanent fixture, or other object, outside any of the lines which bound his opponent's Court (except as provided in Rule 24 (a) and (c)); or
(c) He volley the ball and fail to make a good return even when standing outside the Court; or
(d) He touch or strike the ball in play with his racket more than once in making a stroke; or

EXPLANATION: A player may be deemed to have touched the ball more than once if the ball takes an obvious second trajectory as it comes off the racket, or comes off the racket in such a way that the effect is that of a "sling" or "throw" rather than that of a "hit." Such strokes are informally referred to as "double hits" or "carries." Experienced umpires give the player the benefit of the doubt unless they see such a second trajectory or a definite "second push."

(e) He or his racket (in his hand or otherwise) or anything which he wears or carries touch the net, post (singles stick, if they are in use), cord or metal cable, strap or band, or the ground within his opponent's Court at any time while the ball is in play *(touching a pipe support running across the court at the bottom of the net is interpreted as touching the net);* or
(f) He volley the ball before it has passed the net; or
(g) The ball in play touch him or anything that he wears or carries, except his racket in his hand or hands; or

Note that this loss of point occurs regardless of whether the play is inside or outside the bounds of his court when the ball touches him. A player is considered to be "wearing or carrying" anything that he was wearing or carrying at the beginning of the point during which the touch occurred.

(h) He throws his racket at and hits the ball.

EXAMPLE: Player has let racket go out of his hand clearly before racket hits ball, but the ball rebounds from his racket into proper court. This is not a good return; player loses point.

Case 1. In delivering a first service which falls outside the proper court, the Server's racket slips out of his hand and flies into the net. Does he lose the point?

Decision. If his racket touches the net while the ball is in play, the Server loses the point (Rule 20 (e)).

Case 2. In serving, the racket flies from the Server's hand and touches the net before the ball has touched the ground. Is this a fault, or does the player lose the point?

Decision. The Server loses the point because his racket touched the net while the ball was in play. (Rule 20 (e)).

Case 3. A and B are playing against C and D. A is serving to D. C touches the net before the ball touches the ground. A fault is then called because the service falls outside the service court. Do C and D lose the point?

Decision. The call "fault" is an erroneous one. C and D have already lost the point before "fault" could be called, because C touched the net while the ball was in play. (Rule 20 (e)).

Case 4. May a player jump over the net into his opponent's court while the ball is in play and not suffer penalty?

Decision. No; he loses the point. (Rule 20 (e)).

Case 5. A cuts the ball just over the net, and it returns to A's side. B, unable to reach the ball, throws his racket and hits the ball. Both racket and ball fall over the net on A's court. A returns the ball outside of B's court. Does B win or lose the point?

Decision. B loses the point. (Rule 20 (e) and (h)).

Case 6. A player standing outside the service court is struck by the service ball before it has touched the ground. Does he win or lose the point?

Decision. The player struck loses the point (Rule 20 (g), except as provided under Rule 14 (a)).

EXPLANATION: The exception referred to is that of a served ball that has touched the net en route into the Receiver's court; in that circumstance it is a let service, not loss of point. Such a let does not annul a previous (first service) fault; therefore if it occurs on second service, the Server has one serve coming.

Case 7. A player standing outside the court volleys the ball or catches it in his hand and claims the point because the ball was certainly going out of court.

Decision. In no circumstance can he claim the point;

(1) If he catches the ball he loses the point under Rule 20 (g).

(2) If he volleys it and makes a bad return he loses the point under Rule 20 (c).

(3) If he volleys it and makes a good return, the rally continues.

RULE 21
(Formerly Rule 19)

Player Hinders Opponent

If a player commits any act either deliberate or involuntary which, in the opinion of the Umpire, hinders his opponent in making a stroke, the Umpire shall in the first case award the point to the opponent, and in the second case order the point to be replayed.

Case 1. Is a player liable to a penalty if in making a stroke he touches his opponent?

Decision. No unless the Umpire deems it necessary to take action under Rule 21.

Case 2. When a ball bounds, back over the net, the player concerned may reach over the net in order to play the ball. What is the ruling if the player is hindered from doing this by his opponent?

Decision. In accordance with Rule 21, the Umpire may either award the point to the player hindered, or order the point to be replayed. (See also Rule 25.)

USTA Interpretation: Upon appeal by a competitor that an opponent's action in discarding a "second ball" after a rally has started constitutes a distraction (hindrance), the Umpire, if he deems the claim valid, shall require the opponent to make some other satisfactory disposition of the ball. Failure to comply with this instruction may result in loss of point(s) or disqualification.

RULE 22

Ball Falling on Line — Good

A ball falling on a line is regarded as falling in the Court bounded by that line.

COMMENT: In matches played without officials, it is customary for each player to make the calls on all balls hit to his side of the net, and if a player cannot call a ball out with surety he should regard it as good.

RULE 23

Ball Touching Permanent Fixture

If the ball in play touch a permanent fixture (other than the net, posts, cord or metal cable, strap or band) after it has hit the ground, the player who struck it wins the point; if before it hits the ground his opponent wins the point.

Case 1. A return hits the Umpire or his chair or stand. The player claims that the ball was going into court.
Decision. He loses the point.

RULE 24

Good Return

It is a good return:
(a) If the ball touch the net, post (singles stick, if they are in use), cord or metal cable, strap or band, provided that it passes over any of them and hits the ground within the Court; or
(b) If the ball, served or returned, hit the ground within the proper Court and rebound or be blown back over the net, and the player whose turn is to strike reach over the net and play the ball, provided that neither he nor any part of his clothes or racket touch the net, post (singles stick), cord or metal cable, strap or band or the ground within his opponent's Court, and that the stroke be otherwise good; or
(c) If the ball be returned outside the post or singles stick, either above or below the level of the top of the net, even though it touch the post or singles stick, provided that it hits the ground within the proper Court; or
(d) If a player's racket pass over the net after he has returned the ball, provided the ball pass the net before being played and be properly returned; or
(e) If a player succeeds in returning the ball, served or in play, which strikes a ball lying in the Court.

Note — If, for the sake of convenience, a doubles court be equipped with singles posts for the purpose of a singles game, then the doubles posts and those portions of the net, cord or metal cable and band outside such singles posts shall be regarded as "permanent fixtures *other than* net, post, strap or band," and therefore *not* posts or parts of the net of that singles game.

A return that passes under the net cord between the singles and adjacent doubles post without touching either net cord, net or doubles post and falls within the area of play, is a good return. (But in doubles this would be a "through" — loss of point.)

Case 1. A ball going out of court hits a net post and falls within the lines of the opponent's court. Is the stroke good?
Decision. If a service; no, under Rule 10 (c). If other than a service; yes, under Rule 24 (a).

Case 2. Is it a good return if a player returns the ball holding his racket in both hands?
Decision. Yes.

Case 3. The Service, or ball in play, strikes a ball lying in the court. Is the point won or lost thereby? (A ball that is touching a boundary line is considered to be "lying in the court.")
Decision. No. Play must continue. If it is not clear to the Umpire that the right ball is returned a let should be called.

Case 4. May a player use more than one racket at any time during play?

Decision. No: the whole implication of the rules is singular.

Case 5. Must a player's request for the removal of a ball or balls lying in the opponent's court be honored?

Decision. Yes, but not while the ball is in play.

RULE 25

Interference

In case a player is hindered in making a stroke by anything not within his control except a permanent fixture of the Court, or except as provided for in Rule 21, the point shall be replayed.

Case 1. A spectator gets into the way of a player, who fails to return the ball. May the player then claim a let?

Decision. Yes, if in the Umpire's opinion he was obstructed by circumstances beyond his control, but not if due to permanent fixtures of the Court or the arrangements of the ground.

Case 2. A player is interfered with as in Case 1, and the Umpire calls a let. The Server had previously served a fault. Has he the right to two services?

Decision. Yes; as the ball was in play, the point, not merely the stroke, must be replayed as the rule provides.

Case 3. May a player claim a let under Rule 25 because he thought his opponent was being hindered, and consequently did not expect the ball to be returned?

Decision. No.

Case 4. Is a stroke good when a ball in play hits another ball in the air?

Decision. A let should be called unless the other ball is in the air by the act of one of the players, in which case the Umpire will decide under Rule 21.

Case 5. If an Umpire or other judge erroneously calls "fault" or "out" and then corrects himself, which of the calls shall prevail?

Decision. A let must be called, unless, in the opinion of the Umpire, neither player is hindered in his game, in which case the corrected call shall prevail.

Case 6. If the first ball served — a fault — rebounds, interfering with the Receiver at the time of the second service, may the Receiver claim a let?

Decision. Yes. But if he had an opportunity to remove the ball from the court and negligently failed to do so, he may not claim a let.

Case 7. Is it a good stroke if the ball touches a stationary or moving object on the court?

Decision. It is a good stroke unless the stationary object came into court after the ball was put into play in which case a "let" must be called. If the ball in play strikes an object moving along or above the surface of the court a "let" must be called.

Case 8. What is the ruling if the first service is a fault, the second service correct, and it becomes necessary to call a let under the provisions of Rule 25 or if the Umpire is unable to decide the point?

Decision. The fault shall be annulled and the whole point replayed.

COMMENT: See Rule 13 and Explanation thereto.

RULE 26

The Game

If a player wins his first point, the score is called *15* for that player; on winning his second point, the score is called *30* for that player; on winning his third point, the score is called *40* for that player, and the fourth point won by a player is scored *game* for that player except as below:

If both players have won three points, the score is called *deuce;* and the next point won by a player is called *advantage for that player.* If the same player wins the next point, he wins the game; if the other player wins the next point the socre is again called *deuce;* and so on until a player wins the two points immediately following the score at deuce, when the game is scored for that player.

COMMENT: In matches played without an umpire the Server should announce, in a voice audible to his opponent and spectators, the set score at the beginning of each game, and (audible at least to his opponent) point scores as the game goes on. Misunderstandings will be averted if this practice is followed.

RULE 27

The Set

A player (or players) who first wins six games wins a set; except that he must win by a margin of two games over his opponent and where necessary a set shall be extended until this margin be achieved. NOTE: See tie breaker.

RULE 28

Maximum Number of Sets

The maximum number of sets in a match shall be 5, or, where women take part, 3.

RULE 29

Rules Apply to Both Sexes

Except where otherwise stated, every reference in these Rules to the masculine includes the feminine gender.

RULE 30

Decisions of Umpire and Referee

In matches where a Chair Umpire is appointed his decision shall be final; but where a Referee is appointed an appeal shall lie to him from the decision of a Chair Umpire on a question of law, and in all such cases the decision of the Referee shall be final.

In matches where assistants to the Chair Umpire are appointed (Line Umpires, Net Umpire, Foot-fault Judge) their decisions shall be final on questions of fact, **except that if, in the opinion of the Chair Umpire, a clear mistake has been made, he shall have the right to change the decision of an assistant or order a let to be played.**

When such an assistant is unable to give a decision he shall indicate this immediately to the Chair Umpire who shall give a decision. When the Chair is unable to give a decision on a question of fact he shall order a let to be played.

In Davis Cup or other team matches where a Referee is on court, any decision can be changed by the Referee, who may also authorize the Chair Umpire to order a let to be played.

The Referee, in his discretion, may at any time postpone a match on account of darkness or the condition of the ground or the weather. In any case of postponement the previous score and previous occupancy of courts shall hold good, unless the Referee and the players unanimously agree otherwise.

RULE 31

Play shall be continuous from the first service till the match be concluded, except that:

(a) After the third set, or when women take part the second set, either player is entitled to a rest, which shall not exceed 10 minutes, or, in countries situated between Latitude 15 degrees north and Latitude 15 degrees south, 45 minutes, and except further that when necessitated by circumstances not within the control of the players the Chair Umpire may suspend play for such a period as he may consider necessary.

If play be suspended and be not resumed until a later day the rest may be taken only after the third set (or when women take part the second set) of play on such later day, completion of an unfinished set being counted as one set.

If play be suspended and not resumed until 10 minutes have elapsed in the same day, the rest may be taken only after three consecutive sets have been played without interruption (or when women take part two sets), completion of an unfinished set being counted as one set.

Any nation is at liberty to modify this previous or omit it from its regulations governing tournaments, matches or competition held in its own country, other than the International Tennis Championships (Davis Cup and Federation Cup).

(b) Play shall never be suspended, delayed or interfered with for the purpose of enabling a player to recover his strength or his breath.

(c) A maximum of 30 seconds shall elapse from the end of one point to the time the ball is served for the next point, except that when changing ends a maximum of one minute 30 seconds shall elapse from the last point of one game to the time when the ball is served for the first point of the next game.

NOTE: The USTA interpretation of the reference to 30 seconds in the above paragraph (new as of mid-1978) is that it is not intended to make it possible for a player who wants to slow the between-points pace of a match exaggeratedly, as a gamesmanship or tactical maneuver, to persistently use almost all of the 30 seconds maximum without liability to being found in violation of the "play shall be continuous" principle; and that a Chair Umpire who makes such a finding should be empowered to require the player to play at a reasonable tempo under the prevailing temperature conditions.

These provisions shall be strictly construed. The Chair Umpire shall be the sole judge of any suspension, delay or interference and after giving due warning he may disqualify the offender.

ITF Note: A tournament committee has discretion to decide the time allowed for a warmup period prior to a match. It is recommended that this not exceed five minutes.

USTA Rules Regarding Rest Periods in Age-Limited Categories:

Regular MEN'S and WOMEN'S, and MEN'S 21 and WOMEN'S 21 — Paragraph A of Rule 31 applies, except that a tournament using tiebreakers may eliminate rest periods provided advance notice is given.

BOYS' 18 — All matches in this division shall be best of three sets with NO REST PERIOD, except that in interscholastic, state, sectional and national championships the FINAL ROUND may be best-of-five. If such a final requires more than three sets to decide it, a rest of 10 minutes after the third set is mandatory. Special Note: In severe temperature-humidity conditions a Referee may rule that a 10-minute rest may be taken in a Boys' 18 best-of-three. However, to be valid this must be done before the match is started, and as a matter of the Referee's independent judgment.

BOYS' 16, 14 and 12, and GIRLS' 18, 16, 14 and 12 — All matches in these categories shall be best of three sets. A 10-minute rest before the third set is MANDATORY in Girls' 12, 14 and 16, and in Boys' 12 and 14. The rest period is OPTIONAL in Girls' 18 and Boys' 16. (Optional means at the option of any competitor).

All SENIOR divisions (35's, 40's, 45's, 50's and up), and Father-and-Son: Under conventional scoring, all matches best-of-three, with rest period optional.

When 'NO-AD' SCORING IS USED IN A TOURNAMENT . . . A tournament committee may stipulate that there will be no rest periods, even in some age divisions where rest periods would be optional under conventional scoring. These divisions are: regular Men's (best-of-five) and Women's

. . . Men's 21 (best-of-five) and Women's 21 . . . Men's 35 . . . Seniors (men 45 and over) . . . Father-and-Son.

N.B. Two conditions of this stipulation are: (1) Advance notice must be given on entry blanks for the event, and (2) The Referee is empowered to reinstate the normal rest periods for matches played under unusually severe temperature-humidity conditions; to be valid, such reinstatement must be announced before a given match or series of matches is started, and be a matter of the Referee's independent judgment.

COMMENT: When a player competes in an event designated as for players of a bracket whose rules as to intermissions and length of match are geared to a different physical status, the player cannot ask for allowances based on his or her age, or her sex. For example, a female competing in an intercollegiate (men's) varsity team match would not be entitled to claim a rest period in a best-of-three-sets match unless that were the condition under which the team competition was normally held.

Case 1. A player's clothing, footwear, or equipment becomes out of adjustment in such a way that it is impossible or undesirable for him to play on. May play be suspended while the maladjustment is rectified?

Decision. If this occurs in circumstances not within the control of the player, of which circumstances the Umpire is the sole judge, a suspension may be allowed.

Case 2. If, owing to an accident, a player is unable to continue immediately, is there any limit to the time during which play may be suspended?

Decision. No allowance may be made for natural loss of physical condition. Consideration may be given by the Umpire for accidental loss of physical ability or condition.

COMMENT: Case 2 refers to an important distinction that should be made between a disability caused by an accident during the match, and disability attributable to fatigue, illness or exertion (examples: cramps, muscle pull, vertigo, strained back). Accidental loss embodies actual injury from such mishaps as collision with netpost or net, a cut from a fall, contact with chair or backstop, or being hit with a ball, racket or other object.

Even in case of accident, no more than three minutes should be spent in diagnosis/ prognosis, and if bandaging or medication is going to require more than that, the decision as to whether any additional time is to be allowed should be reached by the Referee after considering the recommendation of the Chair Umpire; and, of course, taking into account the need for being fair to the non-injured player. In no case should the injured player be permitted to leave the court area, nor should more than approximately 15 minutes elapse before either play is resumed or a default declared.

(In Grand Prix matches the Chair Umpire "may allow a one-time, 3-minute rest for accidental injury," but "play must resume in 3 minutes.")

Case 3. During a doubles game, may one of the partners leave the court while the remaining partner keeps the ball in play?

Decision. Yes, so long as the Umpire is satisfied that play is continuous within the meaning of the rules, and that there is no conflict with Rules 36 and 37. (See Case 1 of Rule 36).

NOTE: When a match is resumed following an interruption necessitated by weather conditions, it is allowable for the players to engage in a "re-warm-up" period. It may be of the same duration as the warm-up allowed at the start of the match; may be done using the balls that were in play at the time of the interruption, and the time for the next ball change shall not be affected by this.

RULE 32

Coaching

During a match a player may not receive any coaching or advice, except that when a player changes ends he may receive instruction from a Captain who is sitting on the Court in a team competition.

NOTE: Since the ITF did not stipulate any specific penalty for violations of this rule it appears that a Chair Umpire could do little more than admonish the person doing the forbidden coaching and direct him to cease and desist forthwith. The person's failure to follow this directive could be dealt with under Paragraph 9-a of the USTA Tournament Regulations, which says that "violation of this rule (32) may render the player or his adviser liable to disciplinary action, which may include disqualification of the player or removal of the adviser from the court area."

RULE 33

Ball Change Error
In cases where balls are changed after an agreed number of games, if the balls are not changed in the correct sequence the mistake shall be corrected when the player, or pair in the case of doubles, who should have served with the new balls is next due to serve.

THE DOUBLES GAME

RULE 34

The above Rules shall apply to the Doubles Game except as below.

RULE 35

Dimensions of Court
For the Doubles Game the Court shall be 36 feet (10.97m) in width, i.e. 4½ feet (1.37m) wider on each side than the Court for the Singles Game, and those portions of the singles sidelines which lie between the two service lines shall be called the service sidelines. In other respects, the Court shall be similar to that described in Rule 1, but the portions of the singles sidelines between the baseline and the service line on each side of the net may be omitted if desired.

Case 1. In doubles the Server claims the right to stand at the corner of the court as marked by the doubles side line. Is the foregoing correct or is it necessary that the Server stand within the limits of the center mark and the singles side line?
Decision. The Server has the right to stand anywhere between the center mark and the doubles sideline.

RULE 36

Order of Service
The order of serving shall be decided at the beginning of each set as follows:
The pair who have to serve in the first game of each set shall decide which partner shall do so and the opposing pair shall decide similarly for the second game. The partner of the player who served in the first game shall serve in the third; the partner of the player who served in the second game shall serve in the fourth, and so on in the same order in all subsequent games of a set.

EXPLANATION: It is not required that the order of service, as between partners, carry over from one set to the next. Each team is allowed to decide which partner shall serve first for it, in each set. This same option applies with respect to the order of receiving service.

Case 1. In doubles, one player does not appear in time to play, and his partner claims to be allowed to play single-handed against the opposing players. May he do so?
Decision. No.

RULE 37

Order of Receiving
The order of receiving the service shall be decided at the beginning of each set as follows:
The pair who have to receive the service in the first game shall decide

which partner shall receive the first service, and that partner shall continue to receive the first service in every odd game, throughout that set. The opposing pair shall likewise decide which partner shall receive the first service in the second game and that partner shall continue to receive the first service in every even game throughout that set. Partners shall receive the service alternately throughout each game.

EXPLANATION: The receiving formation of a doubles team may not be changed during a set; only at the start of a new set. Partners must receive throughout each set on the same sides of the court which they originally select when the set began. The first Server is not required to receive in the right court; he may select either side, but must hold this to the end of the set.

Case 1. Is it allowable in doubles for the Server's partner to stand in a position that obstructs the view of the Receiver?

Decision. Yes. The Server's partner may take any position on his side of the net in or out of the court that he wishes. (The same is true of the Receiver's partner).

RULE 38

Service Out of Turn

If a partner serve out of his turn, the partner who ought to have served shall serve as soon as the mistake is discovered, but all points scored, and any faults served before such discovery shall be reckoned. If a game shall have been completed before such discovery the order of service remains as altered.

RULE 39

Error in Order of Receiving

If during a game the order of receiving the service is changed by the receivers it shall remain as altered until the end of the game in which the mistake is discovered, but the partners shall resume their original order of receiving in the next game of that set in which they are receivers of the service.

RULE 40

Ball Touching Server's Partner Is Fault

The service is a fault as provided for by Rule 10, or if the ball served touch the Server's partner or anything he wears or carries; but if the ball served touch the partner of the Receiver or anything which he wears or carries, not being a let under Rule 14 (a), before it hits the ground, the Server wins the point.

RULE 41

Ball Struck Alternately

The ball shall be struck alternately by one or other player of the opposing pairs, and if a player touches the ball in play with his racket in contravention of this Rule, his opponents win the point.

EXPLANATION: This means that, in the course of making one return, only one member of a doubles team may hit the ball. If both of them hit the ball, either simultaneously or consecutively, it is an illegal return. The partners themselves do not have to "alternate" in making returns. (Mere clashing of rackets does not make a return illegal, if it is clear that only one racket touched the ball.)

Should any point arise upon which you find it difficult to give a decision or on which you are in doubt as to the proper ruling, immediately write, giving full details, to John Stahr, U.S.T.A. Rules Interpretation Committee, 65 Briarcliff Rd., Larchmont, N.Y. 10538, and full instructions and explanations will be sent you.

CHAPTER 16

OFFICIALS AND OFFICIATING

The responsibility of officials at tennis events is not easy. Most often they are a carefully selected group of dedicated men and women who have a deep interest in the sport. They often sacrifice their desire to watch the game from the grandstand to serve in an official position on the court. Their job is not an easy one, for they sometimes are harassed by spectators or players, and being human, they can make an occasional mistake. However, abuse and mistakes are relatively rare, and the official enjoys a position of importance and serves as an instrument of smooth match operation.

There are three types of officials used in tournament matches. They are (1) The Referee (2) The Umpire and (3) The Linesman. Each has separate responsibilities. These three positions are discussed in detail below:

THE REFEREE

Appointed by the Tournament Committee. The Referee shall be a member of the committee.

Shall make the draw, assisted by the committee.

Supervise all aspects of play, including conduct of players, umpires, ball boys, grounds crew, etc.

Shall appoint a deputy when he is away from his post.

May default players for reasonable causes. Acts as final judge on appeals of defaulted players.

Schedule matches, assign courts, suspend play, etc., according to conditions.

In summation, is in **total control of the tournament.**

Chair umpire

Linesman

Net umpire

THE UMPIRE (Chair Umpire)

Shall conduct the match according to the rules of tennis.

Shall assume the duties of all linesmen not present.

May ask for the replacement of linesmen if needed.

Sees that players on his/her court follow all rules of match play.

May order a replay of a point if linesmen are unable to make a call.

Shall advise the Referee of unfavorable court or match conditions.

Shall decide any point of law (rules) concerning the match.

May default a player for cause.

THE LINESMAN (Line Umpire)

Calls all shots relating to the lines he is assigned. His decisions are FINAL.

Shall promptly indicate by unsighted signal when he is unable to make a call.

Shall only at the chair umpire's request render a firm opinion on a shot he observed in an area outside his responsibility.

Shall call foot faults pertaining to his line, as outlined in the Rules.

The only other official found on the court is the net umpire, who's primary responsibility is to call a "let" serve. This person may also keep an additional score card as a back-up to the chair umpire.

Thus, we see that as an organized sport, a logical chain-of-command is used to assure a smooth, efficiently run athletic event. This is assured by selecting knowledgeable, qualified and experienced personnel to assist the tournament committee in the organization and administration of the tournament. An experienced player should know and recognize the responsibilities of all tournament officials. This will help him appreciate their responsibilities. They are, after all, working for the players.

TOURNAMENT CHAIN OF COMMAND

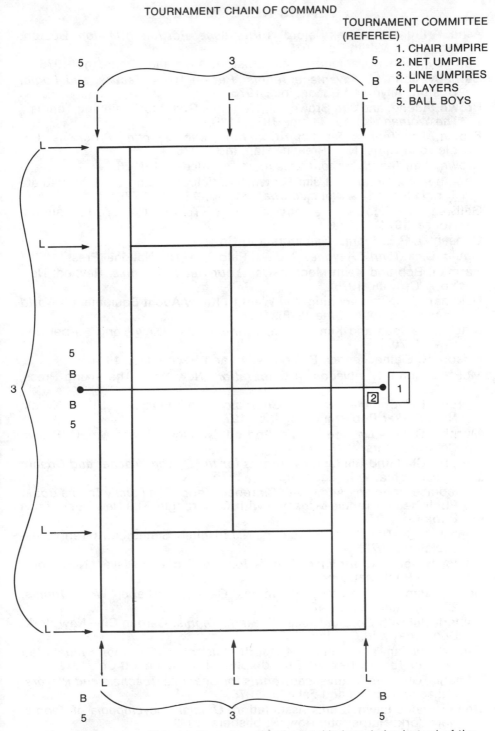

TOURNAMENT COMMITTEE
(REFEREE)
1. CHAIR UMPIRE
2. NET UMPIRE
3. LINE UMPIRES
4. PLAYERS
5. BALL BOYS

In singles, the linesmen will be positioned on the singles side boundaries instead of the doubles sidelines.

TENNIS REFERENCES

Ashe, Arthur with Frank Deford. *Arthur Ashe: Portrait in Motion.* Boston: Houghton Mifflin Co., 1975.

Barnaby, John. *Advantage Tennis.* Boston: Allyn and Bacon, Inc. 1975.

Barnaby, John M. *Advantage Tennis: Racket Work, Tactics, and Logic.* Boston: Allyn and Bacon, Inc., 1975.

Brown, Arlene, and Jim Brown. "A Woman's Guide to Beginning Tennis." *The Woman,* 10, no. 2 (June 1975), 110.

Brown, Jim. *Tennis: Teaching, Coaching, and Directing Programs.* Englewood Cliffs, N.J.: Prentice-Hall, Inc., 1976.

Brown, Jim. *Tennis Without Lessons."* Prentice-Hall, 1978.

Chamberlain, Brian, and Jim Brown. "Anticipation and the Intermediate Tennis Player," *Athletic Journal,* 51, no. 9 (May 1972), 38.

Gallwey, W. Timothy. *The Inner Game of Tennis.* New York: Random House, 1974.

Gensemer, R.E. *Tennis,* Saunders and Co.

Gould, Dick. *Tennis Anyone?* 2nd ed. Palo Alto: The National Press, 1971.

Harman, Bob and Keith Monroe. *Use Your Head in Tennis.* Rev. ed. New York: Crowell, 1975.

Heldman, Julie. "Everything You Want to Know About Equipment," *World Tennis,* 21, no. 1 (June 1973), 16.

King, Billie Jean and Kim Chapin. *Tennis to Win.* New York: Harper and Row, 1970.

Mason, R. Elaine. *Tennis.* Boston: Allyn and Bacon, Inc., 1974.

McPhee, John. *Wimbledon: A Celebration.* New York: The Viking Press, 1972.

Murphy, Bill. *Complete Book of Championship Tennis Drills.* West Nyack, N.Y.: Parker Publishing Co., Inc., 1975.

Murphy, Chet. *Advanced Tennis.* 2nd ed. Dubuque, Iowa: Wm. C. Brown Co. Publishers, 1976.

Murphy, Chet and Bill Murphy. *Tennis for the Player, Teacher and Coach.* Philadelphia: W.B. Saunders Co., 1975.

Newcombe, John and Angie with Clarence Mabry. *The Family Tennis Book.* Published by Tennis Magazine with Quadrangle. The New York Times Book Co., 1975.

Powell, Nick. *The Code.* Princeton, N.J.: United States Lawn Tennis Association, 1974.

Ramo, Simon. *Extraordinary Tennis for the Ordinary Player.* New York: Crown Publishers, Inc., 1970.

Segura, Pancho, and Gladys Heldman. "Getting in Shape," *World Tennis,* 23, no. 2 (July 1975), 48.

Talbert, Bill with Gordon Greer. *Weekend Tennis.* Garden City, New York: Doubleday and Co., Inc., 1970.

Talbert, William and Editors of Sports Illustrated. *The Sports Illustrated Book of Tennis.* Rev. ed. Philadelphia: J.B. Lippincott Co., 1972.

Tilmanis, Gundars A. *Advanced Tennis for Coaches, Teachers and Players.* Philadelphia: Lea and Febiger, 1975.

United States Lawn Tennis Association. *Official Encyclopedia of Tennis.* New York: Harper and Row, Publishers, 1972.

United States Tennis Association. *USTA Official Yearbook.* 51 E. 42nd Street, New York, N.Y., 10017.

Xanthas, P. and Joan Johnson. *Tennis.* Brown and Co., 1976.

MAGAZINES

Tennis Illustrated, Published monthly by the Devonshire Publication Co., 630 Shatto Place, Los Angeles, Ca. 90005.

Tennis Industry. Industry Publishers, Inc., 14961 N.E. 6th Ave., North Miami, Florida 33161.

Tennis, Magazine of the Racquet Sports. Official monthly publication of the USPTA. Published by Tennis Features, Inc., 297 Westport Ave., Norwalk, Conn. 06856.

Tennis. 1255 Portland Place; Boulder, Colorado 80302.

Tennis World. Royal London House, 171B High Street, Beckenham, Kent, BR3 1BY, England.

World Tennis Magazine. Box 3, Grace Station, New York, N.Y. 10028

FILMS

"Anyone for Tennis" (color). USTA, 51 East 42nd Street, New York, NY 10017.

"Beginning Tennis." All-American Productions, P.O. Box 91, Greeley, Co. 80632.

"Beginning Tennis" (color). The Athletic Institute, 805 Merchancise Mart, Chicago, IL 60654.

"Elementary Fundamentals" (b & w, color). All-American Productions, P.O. Box 91, Greeley, CO 80632.

"Elementary Tennis" (color, 15 min.). Dennis Van der Meer, World Tennis, Box 3, Gracie Station, New York, NY 10028.

"Fundamentals of Tennis" (b&w). University of Arizona, Tucson, AZ 85721.

"Great Moments in the History of Tennis." American Safety Razor Co., Philip Morris, Inc., 100 Park Avenue, New York, NY 10017.

"The How To's of Tennis." Wheaties Sports Federation, Title Insurance Bldg., Minneapolis, MN 55401

"Intermediate and Advanced Fundamentals" (b&w, color). All-American Productions, P.O. Box 91, Greeley, CO 80632.

"Intermediate and Advanced Tennis" (b&w). T.N. Rogers Productions, 6641 Clearsprings Rd., Santa Susana, CA 93063.

"Tennis Class Organization" (color, 25 min.). USTA, 51 East 42nd Street, New York, NY 10017.

"Tennis for Beginners" (b&w, color). USTA, 51 East 42nd Street, New York, NY 10017.

"Tennis for Everybody" (b&w, color). Allegro Film Production, 201 West 52nd Street, New York, NY 10019.

"Tennis Fundamentals" (color). Tennis Films International, Inc. 137 Newbury Street, Boston, MA 02116.

"Tennis — A Game of a Lifetime" (b&w, 19 min.). USTA, 51 East 42nd Street, New York, NY 10017.

"Tennis — Sport of a Lifetime." Part One: Class Organization (color, 30 min). Youth Tennis Foundation of Southern California, 609 West Cahuenga Blvd., Los Angeles, CA 90028.

"Tennis Techniques" (color, 12 min). T.N. Rogers Productions, 6641 Clearsprings Road, Santa Susana, CA 93063.

"The Way to Wimbledon" (b&w, color, 20 min). British Information Services, 45 Rockefeller Plaza, New York 10020.